TRANSFORMING THE SOUL

Beyond Soul Retrieval and Integration

MARY PHYLLIS HORN

TRANSFORMING THE SOUL

Beyond Soul Retrieval and Integration

BY

MARY PHYLLIS HORN
M.Ed., Shaman, Rev., Certified Therapist

LIVING LIGHT PUBLISHERS
24 Creekside Circle
Pittsboro, NC 27312

FIRST EDITION copyright 1999, SECOND EDITION copyright 2000: *Finishing Up All Lives On The Planet, using soul retrieval integration methods.* ISBN 0-9709168-0-9

THIRD EDITION copyright 2000: *SOUL INTEGRATION: A Shamanic Path To Freedom And Wholeness.* ISBN 0-9709168-1-7
TX5200617 2000
TX5168462 2000

LIBRARY OF CONGRESS CATALOGUING-IN-PUBLICATION DATA
Horn, Mary Phyllis. 1939-
TRANSFORMING THE SOUL Beyond Soul Retrieval and Integration
    By Mary Phyllis Horn.
    Includes bibliographical references
    ISBN 978-0-9709168-4-6

    1. Shamanism   2. Soul Retrieval.
    3. Hypnotherapy – Spiritual.   4. Metaphysics.
    5. Transpersonal Psychology.   6. New Age.
    7. Spiritual Self Help.
    I. Title.

Printed in the U.S.A.

Living Light Publications
24 Creekside Circle
Pittsboro, NC 27312

Dedication

To The Future

ACKNOWLEDGEMENTS

Much gratitude goes to all of my clients who consented to have their stories and transformation sessions reported in this book. Their beautiful work brings clarity to the use of the various healing methods and principles divulged here. (All Case Studies cite their aliases rather than their real names, for confidentiality reasons.)

Special thanks goes to Barbs Burman for her invaluable help in rewriting this book. Her intuitive insights and adeptness with editing were right on target in helping me hone in on what my heart has wanted to convey all along, as well as what is really important to include in this book.

Most of all, deepest gratitude goes to Spirit, i.e., Divine Source, my High Self, Spirit Teachers and Spirit Helpers, for their faithful support, encouragement, and persistent insistence that I write and again rewrite this material.

COVER ART

The cover of this book is a two-part personal painting given to me by my Spirit Teacher, in a vision. It depicts the human etheric web. In 1996 Spirit first told me that this web holds and organizes the soul, so that we have easy access to all of our spiritual qualities. The back cover is based on a sacred geometry design of the etheric web. The front cover shows the petals of the soul filling in the strands of the web, as it is intended to do. The central bright core depicts the core of one's being.

TRANSFORMING THE SOUL
Beyond Soul Retrieval and Integration

TABLE OF CONTENTS

PREFACE

Welcome! It is no coincidence that you are reading this book. You have been attracted to it due to your quest. Likewise I have been impelled to share this information in this way, in order to help you. Whether or not you have prior knowledge about soul retrieval or soul transformation, your intuition is guiding you to this subject. Come along with me as I tell you my own experience with this wondrous healing tool.

Beyond the initial training in how to do soul retrievals, all the integration information you find in this book was a direct gift to me by my own Spirit Teacher (guiding angel who appears as human, to the mind's eye). The intention initially was for my own healing and spiritual growth. There were no other humans who could help me attain the level of inner integration, i.e., transformation, that my Spirit Teacher said was needed. In fact, there were several who said that a soul retrieval doesn't need inner work, that all a person needs to do is to just continue working on their issues. In the beginning I tried doing that but found myself becoming more deeply mired in the negativity of my soul parts. When I first set up my private practice I also witnessed how two of my clients treated their soul parts in such an uncaring, thoughtless way. It was clear to me that they did not fully grasp their soul parts' significance. All of this disturbed me in such a way that I just had to write down, in book form, what Spirit's guidance has been at each stage of the transformation process.

As I applied Spirit's lessons in my life, I experienced greater wholeness and much wonder, joy and peace. These wonderful feelings gave me the additional overwhelming desire to share with others what I found. My clients too encountered the same healing results, each in their own way, of course. Indeed, the information *is universal* in application. And that is the underlying reason why I have written this book: so that you too may benefit from the insights and methods given here.

GLOSSARY OF SHAMANIC TERMINOLOGY

This Glossary is arranged according to category rather than alphabetically. In this way it is easier to more quickly learn and understand the terminology used in this book.

Shamanism

Shamanism is the spiritual practice ascribed to tribal cultures worldwide that we often think of as based in the psychic and holistic: readings, spiritual healing, communicating with animals and plants telepathically, soul retrieval, carrying the deceased's spirit to the Light, finding where there is game/food, prophecy, finding past causes of current problems, and much more. Each tribe has a specific set of spiritual beliefs and ceremonial practices interwoven with what the shaman does for the tribe. Outwardly, tribes around the world differ widely from each other, yet all shamans get similar results with their people.

Shaman. A tribal person, raised in that tribe's traditions, who has the skills to work with Spirit in the healing ways indicated in the previous paragraph.

Core Shamanism: the core of what all shamanic cultures worldwide do for their people. However, there is no specific religion nor style of ceremonies connected to core shamanism. Practitioners bring to it their own religions and practices.

Shamanic Practitioner: a human who practices various aspects of core shamanism, such as those delineated under "shamanism" above. However, this skilled individual is not connected with a specific tribe.

Spirit Guides

Spirit Guides: beings, usually of the kingdom of angels, who are assigned by highest Spirit to guide and guard us. A few deceased humans may be assigned by highest Spirit to serve as spirit guides, but this is not the norm.

Glossary

Kingdom of Angels: This is a different yet parallel evolutionary path to that of Humans. The angelic kingdom is invisible to the naked eye because of being in a dimension that vibrates so fast that it cannot be experienced through physical senses.

Spirit Teachers: the shamanic term corresponding to spirit guides who usually appear in human form, to the mind's eye.

Power Animals: spirit guides who appear as animals, to the mind's eye. These animals are at least as intelligent as we are and are highly spiritual.

Spirit Helpers: "catch-all" term for spirit guides, spirit teachers, power animals, angels.

Spirit

Spirit: my term for God, Creator, Allah, and/or any other term you may choose to delineate highest Spirit.

High Self: a Hawaiian shamanism term that equates to a personal God who watches over us and is the guiding force for us and our spirit guides.

Soul: our unique self or essence, given to us by highest Spirit. No one else's soul can substitute for it. The soul has a spirit but is not the same as spirit. The Greeks call the soul "psyche" and the spirit "pneuma."

Shamanic Realms & Tools

Shamanic Rattle: a rattle similar in appearance to that used in musical performance. In this case, however, it is used for shamanic rituals.

Upper, Middle and Lower Worlds: the three parallel dimensions used in shamanism. The middle world is where we live in the physical and in our minds, generally. The upper world inwardly looks like sky and clouds and is where the spirit teacher lives. The lower world inwardly looks like our pristine wilderness and is where the power animal lives. (Note: the lower world is not "hell". Shamans say if there is a "hell" it is in the middle world.)

Ordinary Reality: the physical form of Middle world.

Non-Ordinary Reality: that part of the Middle world where we think, pray, create, meditate, go into trance. The upper and lower worlds also are part of non-ordinary reality.

Shamanic Journey: a form of trance using a fast monotonous rhythm, as with rattle or drum, to take the mind into deeper

Glossary

levels; there is inner imagery of actually traveling somewhere. The journey accesses our spirit helpers in the non-ordinary reality of the upper, middle and lower worlds.

Brain Waves of Beta, Alpha, Theta: Scientific laboratories have discovered that the brain generates different types of wavelengths depending upon our inner focus. Beta occurs when we are in decision-making, actively conscious mode. Alpha occurs when we are in a light state of trance akin to being creative or watching an interesting movie. Theta is a deep trance level of rich imagery, like when we are on the verge of sleep and dreaming but know we are awake. Shamanic Journeying makes use of the Alpha and Theta brain-waves.

Foundational Leaders of Core Shamanism

Michael Harner is an American anthropologist who first introduced the practice of core shamanism to our modern society.

The Foundation for Shamanic Studies (FSS) was founded by **Michael Harner.** Its website is www.shamanism.org/

Sandra Ingerman, former educational director for the Foundation for Shamanic Studies (FSS), was the first to bring soul retrieval to the world's awareness. Her book "Soul Retrieval, Mending the Fragmented Self" is a classic in the field of shamanism. At the writing of this book, she is the sole teacher of soul retrieval for FSS.

INTRODUCTION

Soul Retrieval is becoming increasingly well known, yet vital aspects of its integration process are misunderstood and left unaddressed. To address these areas, this book reveals new insights into the true nature of the soul, soul loss, soul retrieval and the unique needs of the soul during its integration and transformation process. My spirit helpers gave me the insights and methods revealed here. They have proved to be applicable and valuable to many people even though originally intended to help only my own personal healing.

Purpose of This Book

This book is specifically for those of you who feel an inner yearning to reclaim all parts of yourself and to bring yourself into complete wholeness. This yearning may take any form: freedom to be yourself, release of fear, oneness with Spirit, comfort in "your own skin" and with life, feeling safe and joyful, or any other expression of healing. Merely obtaining a soul retrieval alone will not necessarily bring you to the resolution of your yearning. The transformation processes described in this book *will* set you on that path, though.

These methods were given to me by Spirit and are intended for use within a shamanic journey or a hypnotherapy trance, primarily because of my own background. I am a life-long musician and artist. I am used to functioning in life from the stance of an altered state of awareness, i.e., predominantly from the alpha mind-state of light trance. It is natural for me to receive information from Spirit while I am physically active, as in walking, painting, playing an instrument or conducting a choir. Because that mind-state seems so commonly ordinary to me, I can make decisions within it as well as question any guidance given by others and Spirit.

The first few years these methods were given to me, middle world ceremonies designed to bring deeper integration had no effect on me. This was because they did not feel deep, due to the reasons given directly above. I literally *needed* the profound

Introduction

depth found in shamanic journeying to the upper and lower worlds, in order to accept the guidance and wisdom of Spirit. As I retrieved and integrated more and more of my own soul parts and grew closer to wholeness, my way of working has changed somewhat. It is now easier to do more processing in middle world non-ordinary reality. A lot of that is due to being very familiar and comfortable with the processes reported in this book.

During the years in which I used only journeying for personal transformation, I found that other people also benefited with that form of work...even those who had good communication with their soul parts within a meditative state. Many were amazed at the increased depth of feeling, understanding and transformation attainable through these methods, compared to the meditative state. These methods work energetically at very deep levels. They help a soul part to fully heal and transform all levels of our being within a month or two of active work in all three worlds.

What I share with you in this book is what I wish someone had known to help me with when I received my first soul retrievals. I went through a lot of struggle, turmoil, "hit and miss" attempts, and a near-miss repeat-soul-loss. I wrote this book in order to help you to not have to go through all that, i.e., to make your process quicker, easier and more satisfying.

Over the years, my process has become increasingly more streamlined and at times more specifically detailed. This allows for people's varying needs. In other words, not all of the methods in this book will be used in any *one* soul retrieval. With multiple soul retrievals, you will probably find yourself using some methods one time and skipping over them on another occasion. As you allow your own spirit helpers to help you, your experience will feel fluid and natural.

Your ultimate benefit will be to have full use of all your soul parts' capabilities at any moment in your life, without the interference of previously limiting habits, beliefs and attitudes. You will also have permanent healing and energy-reclamation in those areas of your life specifically addressed by the returned soul parts.

The Intentions of "Transforming The Soul"

  • *Intention #1:* to share deep insights into the nature of soul loss and the unique, miraculous healing process of soul retrieval and its transformation. The concept of soul retrieval is so new that aspects of it can be confused with other forms of therapy.

Introduction

There is much about the integration process that imitates forms of psychotherapy. "Imitation" does not mean that the returning soul parts will respond favorably to those timeworn forms of treatment. In fact, the truth is exactly the opposite.

Soul retrievals *begin* with a breakthrough, not end with it, as may be the case with other forms of therapy. Other forms work from the outside->in, that is, from the conscious mind inward through emotions and, hopefully, to the mind and Spirit. This is a laborious process that has to contend with personality defenses and emotional turmoil. Conversely, soul retrievals and their transformational process heal from the inside-> out, meaning, from Spirit first. This then filters outward to emotions and the conscious mind. Spirit's powerful yet subtle force swiftly bypasses conscious defenses and gently wipes away emotional blocks, producing quick, lasting change.

On the surface, the immediate after-math of soul retrieval mimics other more traditional forms of therapy. It may seem that all you need is to retrieve a soul part and then merely resume working on your issues, using standard methods. Such is a misunderstanding of what the soul part needs. The soul part considers itself to be in oneness with its particular spiritual quality, not separate from it. It has a personal identification with the quality. Working directly with the soul part, its intelligent awareness and its special spiritual quality, honors it and is an essential component of the process. It is imperative to view and approach each spiritual quality and each feeling as a *person* (soul part), not as a *thing* (spiritual quality).

• *Intention #2:* to share the safe, fast ways that Spirit has given me to transform the soul parts and our selves. These can be done in facilitated sessions, or alone within a shamanic journey or self-induced trance. Methods that work directly with soul transformation are described in this book.

With soul transformation, slow progress is not the safe path. You are dealing with what seems like a newborn quality and energy. The healthy attitude regarding a newborn baby is to attend to it the moment it cries; such helps to give the infant a sense of self-worth and good self-esteem. When a baby cries, the longer you delay coming to its aid, the more it adopts abandonment issues and dysfunctional beliefs. The same is true of newly returned soul parts. If you choose to progress slowly, you neglect the soul part and end up compounding your issues and lowering your self-esteem.

Introduction

Soul transformation needs to progress quickly in order to access, fully and easily, the strengths and traits offered by the soul part in ways that are natural, joyful and functional. Such avoids complications and negative accentuation of emotions, beliefs and attitudes.

My Spirit-gifted insights and methods explain how to work with soul parts more effectively and efficiently to make sure they:
(1) do not cause problems within the totality of you,
(2) strengthen the unity of your soul in general, and
(3) give you the most healing possible from your soul retrieval, beyond the initial burst of newness. The ultimate purpose of these methods is to bring about complete infusion of the new soul parts into you in a way that is free of dysfunctional attitudes, beliefs and habits. They help you to know yourself better, *which is soul retrieval's true purpose!*

• **Intention #3:** Many of these methods can be used for spiritual development, self-healing, inner growth, and transformation that are independent of soul retrievals. They are self-empowering and adaptable to all kinds of healing modalities and inner work. They help produce rapid improvement in optimism and self-esteem, change habits, release dysfunctional beliefs easily, and more fully understand life, self and others. They also help you form a closer bond with Spirit.

These methods are designed for use within a shamanic journey or hypnotherapy session, but also work well for people who know how to go inward and confer freely with the inner self without the use of the journey. Working from a deeply introspective trance state, we are coddled by Spirit and feel profoundly supported, loved and protected. That allows you to easily release negativity and fear. Inner changes that result are personally satisfying and gentle. They lead naturally to outer, behavioral changes.

The end result of all the work given here is full use of your soul part without any resistance from you nor sabotage from the soul part. The soul part is intended to heal, transform and uplift your life in every aspect it is in charge of. Your transformation is intended to be a permanent life-change that helps you feel and act more truly to the best of who you instinctively know you are.

Introduction

Truth-Seeking Beliefs Shape This Work

My personal philosophy of life, Spirit and healing are delineated here, in relation to the transformation work described in this book.

• The spark of the Divine is in everyone and every soul part. We are that divine spark of light. If we have any sense of feeling bad or unworthy, such comes from an illusion probably brought on by life's harsh experiences. Even though we are the spark of Spirit, our more conscious beliefs, attitudes and habits of thought may attempt to sabotage the awareness of such a fact because they are attached to the illusion of limited life-experiences. It is that part of self, not the spark of Spirit within, that still needs to grow into oneness with the Light. In that respect, I believe that all of us can change and grow, if we so choose.

• When we feel pervasive fear, it could be a signal of any number of things: there has been soul loss, or soul loss is about to occur, or it is a deterrent from circumstances that would cause soul loss. In the form of caution, fear can be a natural warning of something being wrong. However, *fear is not us!* It is merely a signal that something is amiss.

• There is always a way to heal a soul part and the self. Only limited thinking gives up before the healing path is found. A creative attitude, aligned with Spirit, helps us find the healing path more easily and quickly.

• There is also always a way to heal quickly and gently. Agonizing is not needed. Agony is the emotional partner to limited thinking; its purpose is to fool us into giving up right before success occurs. It is the "darkest before the dawn." Sometimes there may be exhaustion after a soul-transformation session, yes, but not agony. Exhaustion is a signal that we have worked hard and productively, and that it is now time to rest and assimilate the healing.

• Our spirit helpers are always here to aid us. All that is needed is for us to let them do so.

• Our future is the result of what we choose in the present. Our spirit may give us a mission for the future, but *our free will can choose the timing of that.* It even allows us to choose to not fulfill the mission.

• Shamanically, my primary focus is to teach a sense of community within each human, i.e., creating unification and sacred space within one's self. If there is not full harmony and cooperation among parts of one human, that person cannot attain

Introduction

full harmony and cooperation with other humans. To paraphrase the ancient adage: "As within, so without." That is, whatever we experience within self is what appears in the world around us and in our relationships.

Unique Qualities Of This Book Include:
   • New insights about the soul, soul loss, soul retrieval and transformation. These insights add to what other books have only started to reveal. They delineate the true uniqueness of soul retrieval and its transformation, and how to distinguish it from other forms of therapy.
   • Because some people need different ways of working, I clearly delineate in this book what is principle and what is method. In that way it is easier for you to adapt the principles given, to fit intricately with your own methods.
   • Soul transformation methods previously unknown.
   • Rapid spiritual healing methods previously unknown.
   • Methods for healing the grief involved in releasing long-standing habits and belief patterns.
   • Insights into the nature of resistance and how to side-step it into true, gentle healing.
   • Methods for merging and inter-linking spiritual qualities so that you have instant innate access to all qualities within you, without resistance or blocking.
   • Case studies of clients, illustrating Spirit's methods in action. Throughout this book I will use scenarios to illustrate points being made. These scenarios come from actual case studies of my clients; I will, however, not be using their real names.
   • All methods can be self-done by shamanic journeyers and those adept at self-trance.
   • All methods can be facilitated by therapists schooled in spiritual hypnotherapy or shamanic methods.
   • Methods are applicable to both beginners and the advanced on the spiritual path. All that is needed is the willingness to do the work.

   Enjoy! I am glad you are here. Thank you for following your Spirit's call to explore this work.

Introduction

CHAPTER I

MY SHAMANIC PATH

Signs of the Path

In tribal cultures throughout the world, Shamans are not chosen by genetic heritage the way our western countries have chosen royalty. Rather, they are chosen by Spirit. This choice manifests in various ways, such as in Near-Death Experiences, psychic ability, prophecy, mediumship, gifts of spiritual healing, visions, ability to communicate with animals, spiritual initiations, "big dreams," to name a few. The individual who reports any one of these experiences is immediately taken under the wing of the shaman, to be trained further. Often, the shaman is called "the wounded healer." This means she has to find ways to heal herself, and through doing that, discovers powerful ways to heal others.

Our western culture lost its shamanic path centuries ago. As a result, many children who now report such abilities have been shamed and discounted, rather than helped to develop in a healthy and ethical way. Seemingly, those who are lucky enough to have family members who are interested in metaphysics or have experienced psychic phenomena themselves, have allowed their abilities to survive.

In that respect I was lucky. Both sides of my family have a long history of creativity of all kinds. My mother and her mother had repeated spontaneous psychic experiences. Mom embraced and encouraged any such abilities I had and gently guided me to TV programs and articles on the subject. She was not interested in metaphysics, per se, so she had no way of guiding me to anyone who could help me develop accordingly. But at least she did not discount me for them.

Shamanic Signposts

If I had grown up in a tribal culture, any *one* of the following occurrences I have had would have been sufficient sign for the shaman to set me onto the shamanic path.

Channeling Creativity. I am a life-long musician. During performances I often feel like I am channeling Spirit through the music, working in tandem with the vibration and musical expression of the people present. As a choral conductor I felt I was working with invisible energies, which resulted in a more inspiring musical expression from the singers. I attribute this ability to work with and conduct energies as my preparation for doing soul retrievals and calling on angelic help during depossession work.

Visions. At about age three I clairvoyantly saw a shining, white-robed man who gave me a message of encouragement.

Mediumship Ability. For a few weeks after my mother and brother Jim died in a house fire in 1979 they communicated with me in numerous "visits" which I experienced clairvoyantly. Since that time, when someone I know dies, I can mentally call out, "I am here if you need to talk." Sometimes they come by and sometimes they do not.

"Big" Dreams. "Big" dreams are vivid ones that often carry a strongly spiritual message. Some of mine are precognitive both for myself and for others.

Within a few days after their deaths, my brothers Steve and Rob showed up in my dreams to say goodbye. Years later, Rob came to me in a dream to help me finish an oil painting I was doing of him.

Since 1978, every time I dream about Christmas, someone I know dies. (At least three of the dreams were documented ahead of the fateful events.) All but two did not contain the person's identity, so I could not warn them. Spirit said this was because the person's spirit intended them to leave. Warning them would not have changed the event. The dream was meant only to keep me from being devastated by the loss.

On January 8, 1979, I dreamed of my parents' house-fire (I was in South Carolina and they lived in Pennsylvania) at the exact time it happened. I saw the position of my mother as she succumbed, and I felt the awesome euphoria she experienced as she left her body. Two days later, the firemen found both Mom and Jim at the exact spot I had seen them in the dream. The clothing they were found in also was what I saw in the dream. In the first part of the dream, my witnessing position was a half- story higher than that house's construction; it was as if I were suspended in mid-air. My father rebuilt atop the old foundation; the current house is a half-story higher than the old house!

Initiation Dreams in 1979. During a research project with the Association for Research and Enlightenment (A.R.E.), founded by Edgar Cayce in Virginia Beach, VA, I had a significant dream of the Christ. His deep blue eyes evoked a vibration in me that resonated through every molecule of my body, continuing for a half hour after I woke up.

Throughout that fall my dreams contained many geometrical forms and involved studies within "universities." I was not enrolled in college, and such themes were not the norm for my dreams. Research since then indicates that these themes are common prior to a major spiritual initiation. During this same time period I also began to have *benign* precognitive dreams, for the first time in my life.

Psychic Abilities. Also during the fall of 1979, my psychic abilities increased dramatically: telepathy, remote viewing, clairvoyance, and clairaudience. It was very puzzling, because I was not actively trying to develop them.

Spiritual Initiation. On December 9, 1979, I experienced a major spiritual initiation that started at church. Within my inner awareness, a group of saints or holy ones in Spirit, robed in white, stood before me. One of them put a scepter to the crown of my head while the rest intoned a holy chant. I felt a strong, yet subtle, emanation or vibration that descended into me, pervading my whole body and lasting for nearly seven hours. No one else could see my body vibrating; only I could feel it. One of these holy beings told me of the tests I would be given and the emotional hardships I would go through over the subsequent ten years. He also told me of the beauties of Spirit that would result from it. Then I noticed a deep royal blue color pervading everything I saw, yet it did not change nor distort other colors in any way. This color lasted for six hours.

Intense Interest In Metaphysical Subjects. After that initiation, my interest in metaphysics increased and I took nearly every class that came my way, like a starving person at a smorgasbord. I could not get enough!

My Shamanic Path

Reluctant Shaman

For fifteen years the shamanic path pulled at me incessantly. It simultaneously fascinated and repulsed me, intrigued and bored me. I sensed a profound depth to it but could not discern any details of how to access the heart of it. I tried to study it from books and through workshops with elders of various Native American tribes, but I always came away with a sense of two-dimensions in a three-dimensional metaphysical world.

I also had mistaken beliefs about shamanism, mistaken because of my incomplete knowledge of what it was all about. I saw individual tribes in their traditional costumes doing their tribal ceremonies. None fit into my modern day world. I could not see myself standing in a public high school classroom wearing tribal clothing and performing tribal music.

I heard whispers about communication with spirits and interpreted that as talking with the dead. This frightened me no end, probably because of a scary incident at age five of seeing an ugly ghost hanging onto my alcoholic great-uncle. But perhaps it was also due to my untrained mediumship ability and the easy deception the astral realm can wreak on us.

I heard about worship of the Ancestors and thought, "A dead grandfather is no wiser than a live one. No way can I worship another human. God, only!" I did not realize at that time that "spirits" is another way of saying "angels" and "Ancestor" may include a "Spirit Teacher" in addition to family ancestors.

All the while resisting the shamanic path's beckoning, I delved more deeply into metaphysics. Every class, workshop, retreat and study group on any subject available, you name it, I have probably studied it! My study culminated in ordination at Sancta Sophia Seminary. This interfaith, metaphysical seminary was founded by Carol Parrish, who is part Cherokee. It is located in Tahlequah, Oklahoma, in the middle of the Western Cherokee territory!

My life got more and more turbulent as I continued to resist the shamanic path. Spiritual law says that if we do not obey the call of our soul, the "Lords of Karma" (tests brought by Spirit that feel difficult to withstand) will intensify our lives. Did they ever! A long career teaching high school choral music grew increasingly unsatisfying. I knew I needed to step fully onto the spiritual path, yet fear of the unknown held me back.

Surrendering To The Path

Then one day I had an extremely clear and profound experience: instead of being frightened by the presence of a recently deceased person, I actually sent one on to the Light – successfully, despite not having had instruction on how to do this! That made me realize that I *must* set foot onto the shamanic path no matter what happened. The moment I committed to that path, doors and avenues miraculously opened for me both during the training period and even later when I set up my shamanic counseling/healing practice. Previously, my inner spiritual guidance was "catch as catch can" erratic. Since stepping on the path it finally became resoundingly clearer and more accurate. Over the years, I have felt more at one within myself and with all of creation. My faith in Spirit has multiplied exponentially and this trust has not been betrayed.

The moment I surrendered to the shamanic path, I sought out a professor in graduate school who is a shamanic practitioner and asked him to help me begin the process. My first step was to take the Basic Core Shamanism workshop with anthropologist Michael Harner. The shamanic journeying he taught was "old home week" in familiarity, uncannily similar to Kabalah path-working meditations.

Core Shamanism ethics, like tribal ethics, includes a reverence for the Earth and a respect for all kingdoms in nature, a reverence that has been part of me since birth. There is also a deep grounding, a practicality, about all aspects of core shamanism: grounding in the Earth, in specific safeguards, in respect for spirit helpers, in seriousness of purpose and in insistence on playing out into life the wisdom gained during journeying. I have worked with and towards this all my life. Even in my music career, I felt a need to take what I heard within and convey it outwardly through performance and teaching. Just thinking about doing something is insufficient; it needs to be applied in life.

Wounded? Healer!

I am a wounded healer. That means that I came into my current healing profession by first seeking healing for myself. This life is a karmic one, in which I am clearing up the loose ends of all my other lives on the planet. It requires looking into past causes for current problems. It also has required looking for this life's purpose both for self-healing and for helping others. During all of this retro-focus, Spirit has given me insights and ways to access depths of the human spirit seldom found elsewhere. Spirit also gave me the gift to see, in trance, where others' difficulties are coming from and to help them attain the healing they request.

This life has been blessed with coincidences and serendipity in many ways. Clearly, Spirit has been working hard for me, "behind the scenes." I marvel at how I "just happened onto" the exactly right teachers, musically and spiritually; they were ones with strong integrity who gave well-grounded, practical instruction. The same is true of organizations I became acquainted with throughout my spiritual search, and friends who brought to town the right metaphysically–oriented therapists I needed for further healing. Clearly, Spirit and my spirit helpers have been guiding me along the straight and narrow path of transformation.

During my career as a high school choral music teacher, I often thanked Spirit for allowing me to make a living doing something I loved and that often uplifted me in the midst of it. I also knew that teaching was not the end mission for my life. Rather, it was an all around support while I did my in-depth healing of karmic issues, in preparation for this current mission.

In preparation for this healing mission, I gravitated towards schools that required experiential, altered-state work in addition to intellectual learning: Sancta Sophia Seminary, The Naropa Institute, and the Alchemy Institute of Denver. As a life-long musician, I see it as common sense that a person would not take music lessons from someone who had never learned how to play the instrument. Why, then, go to a counselor who had not experienced therapy?! We best know where someone else is coming from if we first experience it ourselves.

In both music and counseling there is a two-sided rose: As we help others, we better understand our own abilities and selves. As we improve our own abilities and selves, we more fully understand how to help others.

MY FIRST SOUL RETRIEVAL

The first soul retrieval ever done for me was a strong learning experience as to the nature of the integration and transformation processes.

When Terry, my shamanic practitioner, blew my six-month-old soul part (now known as "6M") into me and vaguely described why she left, I knew instantly what he was referring to. I had already recalled the memory of that circumstance, as the result of a breath-work session ten years before.

I came to realize that since birth, 6M had been instrumental in getting me to cry out for my physical needs. Yet I experienced much delay, great frustration and sometimes a lot of panic. My mother was a loving person who exuded an atmosphere of total acceptance of others; people loved being around her. But she had the distorted idea that the way to teach an infant not to be selfish is to let it cry for fifteen to twenty minutes before answering its needs. Albeit well meaning, she did not recognize that an infant cannot do for itself; it must make a sound in order to get someone to tend to it. Fifteen to twenty minutes is an eternity of suffering through a cold wet diaper, an open pin sticking the skin, hunger pangs, a stopped-up nose that can not breathe, or a need for love and attention.

In the actual soul loss incident, 6M had reached the "last straw" of thwarted attempts to effectively stand up for my well-being. She also resonated from a past-life fear that caused her to misperceive the truth of that current life incident. She saw it quite literally as a life and death issue.

I thought I had had full recall of the incident, from the breath-work memories. However, several weeks after the soul retrieval, 6M suddenly called my attention to another part of the scene, one that gave me crucial understanding about the soul loss process. In my breath-work memory I recalled Mom as if I were standing at her height, across the room from her; clearly I was out of body! 6M's "new" memory, one that she had taken with her when she left, was that of being held lovingly by my mother after another interminable wait. I saw her warm smile and felt the soft envelope of love she exuded.

In that scene, 6M was arguing with the rest of me. She was determined to "die" in order to get out of having to put up with all those untenable situations. The rest of me was determined to live. It was a virtual tug-of-war. 6M would not listen to the wisdom part of me. My inner wisdom knew that current incident was actually benign and loving. It also knew what the future held and that all would work out well. But there was no convincing 6M of that, nor would she wait to find out. She just wanted to get out of there! Finally, in despairing resignation, "I" let her go. Instantly, my field of vision dimmed and became hazy; my awareness was less sharply defined than before she left. I was more pliable to my family's wishes for me, regardless of whether my needs were more crucial.

6M's Benefits

The first benefit I gained from the retrieval of 6M was a sense of solidity and inner completeness. On the ride home from the soul retrieval, I felt like I was looking out through golden sunlight, even though it was nine in the evening and the sky was pitch black. The friend who was my witness at the ceremony said I looked stronger, clearer, and more self-assured. What I felt was a growing joy, along with the impression of that fore-mentioned increased inner light.

A month or two later, I suddenly realized that I was making decisions easily. These were not little decisions. They were *BIG!* I changed my focus in graduate school, setting off in an entirely different direction with my intended career, and making major money outlays to attain these. Not only was I making life-changing decisions, I was making them with little to no effort. That naturalness, in itself, was a mind-blower! You see, all my life I had had difficulty with decisions. If the situation were not clear-cut, I would go through an agonizing process that never really ended comfortably, nor could I be sure the decision was the "right one." No amount of decision-making instruction from others made any difference. The newfound ease and naturalness after the soul retrieval were clearly the result of 6M's influence. Bless her!

At the soul retrieval ceremony, Terry said 6M would call back all my other soul parts. Well, several weeks later I tried to do that. In meditation and again in shamanic journeys I mentally sent out the call: "Calling all soul parts! Return to me! Calling all soul parts, return!" I even imagined them coming back, but to no avail. I felt no change. Only after the soul retrieval training with Sandra Ingerman did others of my soul parts begin returning, one at a time.

During this period I was also doing soul retrievals for other people. As I helped them, and myself, heal and integrate, I began to notice signposts regarding whether or not a soul part was fully transformed.

Latch-Key Integration ("Oh Dopey Me!")

When I checked in with Terry a week after the retrieval, he offered to help me get started on integration. At the same time, I was going to a Transpersonal Therapist, fulfilling the mentorship requirement for my graduate studies in Transpersonal counseling Psychology. I felt that she could help me, so I refused Terry's offer. I later came to see my error. My mentor, good as she was at counseling, did not know to focus solely on the returning soul part for the healing. As a result, it took me years to grow this part up to my current age. That should have happened in three months or less.

Two years went by before I recognized the significance of 6M always showing up as a baby when I thought of her or saw her during a shamanic journey! Blind much? Well, I sure was! It is interesting how we can perceive a truth in other people but are oblivious to it within ourselves! I am also very thankful that my work with others provides an avenue to wake up to my own inner self. My clients have been beautiful mirrors for me.

What I did notice was that each time another, older, soul part returned to me, it stirred up emotions relating to 6M. I thought that was because the new soul part had lived through and also recalled the 6M experience. "Oh dopey me!" It was actually 6M clamoring to be heard, just like a toddler does when a new baby comes into the family.

Months(!) later it dawned on me that 6M was still a baby because she had more experiences and strengths to share with me. During that sharing she told me that she could help me stand up for myself in ways and circumstances I had not yet tapped into. As I applied her newly shared strength, she grew up a bit. As I at times "chickened out" into familiar fear, she appeared again as a baby. I had to discern when to be decisive and when to stand up for myself. At the same time I had to balance this with compassion for others or exercise the wisdom to wait for right timing to act. It required the balancing of many inner traits, much like walking a tightrope.

Soul Loss In Progress ("The Scare Of My Life")

In June of 1997, 6M's "standing up for self" gave me quite a scare. For a couple of weeks I was in a deep depression with feelings of despair, hopelessness, and thoughts that "no one appreciates my abilities." Nothing I did lifted this mood. In fact, it got worse to the point that I thought for sure I was truly going to die. As pervasive a feeling as this was, my mind could find no cause for it from anything in my life. People were complimentary, my work was going well, and my diet was healthy. It was a very puzzling situation!

When death thoughts entered, I finally did a shamanic journey to find out the truth of what was going on. The moment I got to the upper world, "standing up for self" split off from me and fled to the nether regions of the lower world. I knew instantly that this was soul loss in progress. I flew after her, pleading, "Don't go! Please come back! I need you and your strengths!" She hesitated, listened to my heartfelt plea, and tentatively came back to discuss the matter.

She expressed outrage at all the times over the previous three years that she strongly urged me to speak out and stand up for myself, but I had refused to do so. I had held her in very tight rein. A flood of memories flitting through my mind illustrated her words. She saw no reason to stay with me. She said I did not appreciate her nor did I prize her abilities. (It was *her* depression and feeling unappreciated that I had been sensing.)

In turn, I told her that at the time of each impulse to speak out, the feelings were explosive and the mental words ferocious. I knew if I vented my feelings in that very way at that time, I would devastate others, both wounding and alienating them. I could not let that happen.

Her readiness to leave made it imperative to find a compromise. Since the only way she knew how to express herself was with explosiveness, she said she would signal me as to when to speak out. Then the parts of me that carry Wisdom and Compassion could do the actual speaking, with love and caring.

The wonders of journeying. I am so grateful for being able to do shamanic journeying! Without it, I would have continued to be oblivious to what was happening; not even meditation was deep enough to be able to discern the truth of what was going on. Within the shamanic journey, my spirit guides step in to deliver the truth in a clear and compassionate way. They were exuding support to me and to my soul part, helping us both to know that there really was hope in our learning how to get along. If I had not been able to do the journeying, my "6M" soul part would have left, taking other assertive parts with her. I would no longer have been as assertive. And, the soul loss would have left behind a pungent residue of low-grade depression, lower self-esteem and feeling unappreciated without knowing why. Soul loss in progress leaves a lasting residue of pain if the soul part is allowed to complete the leaving process. It is *not* a pleasant solution to hardship, if you have any other options.

Deeper Integration

The tandem between 6M, Compassion and Wisdom worked well for a month or so, until it became clear that this was too cumbersome an experience. It was like having to call for a committee meeting before each assertive action...clearly an unwieldy situation! I needed for decisions-to-act to be more instantaneous. Obviously, more healing was needed to achieve a deeper level of cooperation between 6M and my other soul parts, one that resulted in our blending together, i.e., soul-merging.

Basic Principle of Soul-Merging. Soul-merging is not something that can be done at a purely intellectual level. It has to be done at the energetic level, deeply, in trance, as you will read about in a moment. The process requires complete trust between the self and all not-yet-fully-integrated soul parts. There must be the trust that each part has been totally cleared and healed of anything that would lead to wrong action ethically, so as not to find yourself suddenly saying or doing something unwanted. There must be the trust that you are very clear about who you are and what you stand for, in order to keep the boundary clear between yourself and other people. Essentially, this merging of soul parts and self is an issue of trust in Spirit to have done all the clearing and healing necessary, and trust within yourself that all of your soul parts and you have the same values. This last is true, of course, if all the healing has been done.

My Soul-Merging. So, during a shamanic journey to "standing up for myself" I found myself looking at the belief system I held when I was six months old. Wisdom and 6M showed me how they felt, by the way they looked, metaphorically: Wisdom looked whitish and frail, lacking in strength; 6M looked dark, with her head bowed and her body exuding powerfully intense emotion and pain. I held them both loosely within my awareness, as if in my arms, and allowed them to share their concerns. I felt totally open and unconditionally accepting of everything they shared. We opened up to each other to find concurring beliefs as well as the faulty, conflicting ones that needed healing.

I called for healing from my spirit helpers and the Light. They took away the pain, acknowledged the innate purity of each soul part, and validated the needs expressed. I chimed in with a "no nonsense" command that it was time to give up the pain of the past: "Pain is not part of who we are! It is only a rider, a thing to hold. Thoughts of retribution only perpetuate pain. We have to let them go in order to embrace the peace and joy of the present.

It is time to forgive, to release the past to oblivion, and to grasp hold of a new, more peaceful way of being."

I gave them my love and total abiding presence and allowed them to merge with each other. Then they infused into every atom of my being. As each spurt of healing occurred, I felt a surge of soothing, clearing energy pervade pathways of my body. Tendrils of energy shot through habit patterns, changing them and relaxing muscles and tensions relating to them. At the same time, I felt more compassion for and confidence in Wisdom.

Wisdom gave 6M and me her altruistic attitude and expansive life-view. 6M gave Wisdom and me her strength and confidence. She exuded relief at finally being heard. My openness and love gave them both the freedom to go anywhere within my life-experience memories that they needed to in order to affect further change and healing.

I felt my outlook change subtly, surely, at the feeling level without knowing the life-particulars. Occasionally, memories flashed into awareness. When they stayed in mind, I knew to direct healing to them. Sometimes this involved forgiveness, sometimes it required calling in spiritual healing, sometimes I needed to explain to 6M the reasons behind what had transpired, and sometimes it involved a merging process with still another soul part's quality.

Strengthening Factors

This subtle merging of traits is not a conceptual, intellectual process. It is not just a trip into the imagination. *It is an actual merging of soul energy.* The inner strengthening it produces is borne out later through changes in attitude and feelings, and through positive words and actions in life.

On an on-going basis, 6M continued to show me an even subtler level, of integrating her energy into my other soul qualities. Merging with them, she gives them a strength they did not have before.

For example: Merging with compassion, she gives me the courage to reach out to others with love. Previously I would have felt very self-conscious and shy. "Standing up for myself" now has a deeper meaning of daring to stand up for my desire to be compassionate. Another example: Merging with wisdom to wait, she gives me the strength of will, not just the "nice thought," to actually wait for the right time to act.

6M is a primary, pivotal, core soul part. She is very decisive, strengthens all my other traits, and is a unifying factor. I suspect that is what Terry meant when he said 6M would bring back other soul parts. It is now her task to merge with other returning soul parts, to strengthen them and help them grow. Future soul loss is not an option.

Speed of Transformation

The variety of experience, regarding soul transformation speed and ease, seems to have more to do with our issues and the specific soul parts coming back than anything else.

My history of "6M" conveys a very specific picture of one form of the transformation process. Others of my personal soul retrievals integrated and transformed much differently. The following is a totally different experience:

I taught high school choral music for thirty-one years. About five years after I left teaching and had received numerous soul retrievals from my spirit helpers, I had a most amazing experience. On one shamanic journey I saw a long line of "adult me's" coming into me in a rapid stream. My spirit teacher said that I had finished all the personal work I needed to do regarding my teaching years and that the only thing left for total healing was to receive these thirty or more soul parts. He said I would not need to do any integration work regarding them, at that time, and such proved to be true. My sense of self felt more whole and complete after this retrieval; at no time did I feel overwhelmed nor experience separateness with those soul parts.

Nine years later, my spirit teacher told me to then do transformation work with those thirty or more soul parts. When I asked why, he said I had to have welcomed back other soul parts and reached a higher degree of transformation occurred within twenty minutes.

CHAPTER 2

THE TRANSFORMED SOUL: A METAPHOR

Most soul loss has subtle ramifications. Some has as dramatic an effect as in this metaphor. But whether subtle or dramatic, the following is nevertheless a *very close analogy* of the Soul Loss, Soul Retrieval and Transformation process. This metaphor discourse will give you an over-all sense of how the process works.

The italicized portions below describe the physical metaphor. The plain print following it explains how the metaphor relates to the process of Soul Loss-Retrieval-Transformation.

BASIC OVER-VIEW

Soul Loss

Step 1. You suffer the amputation of a foot. This foot is put into a freezer, with all nerve endings intact and openly raw. It stays frozen at the growth level it was in when amputated. It cannot grow nor can it be of any use to you. The soul part, when it separates from the body, remains frozen at the age at which it left. Its feelings remain as alive as if it were in the body, and it can not get beyond obsessing over the reasons why it left. It cannot communicate with you nor can it grow and evolve.

Step 2. Your ankle is aflame with pain. Anyone coming near the wound is seen as a threat to making the pain worse. Just as pain is a general symptom of part of the body being cut off, fear is a general symptom of part of the soul leaving. At the time of soul loss, fear moves in. You perceive it as a powerful deterrent to avoid further trauma.

Step 3. You are at first incapacitated, requiring external help and attention to getting your needs met. It is critical, after a trauma, for you to receive attention and emotional help. If the trauma is not outwardly noticeable, you may instinctively reach out to others for help and attention. For instance, if the soul part took away decisiveness, you may all of a sudden uncharacteristically resort to asking other people for advice.

Step 4. In time, the wound appears to heal. Such is actually numbness, with occasional "phantom" sensations. In suffering soul loss you may experience emotional numbness or a sense of not being quite as alive, as if in a twilight world. You may also occasionally experience unexplainable emotional outbursts, unexplainable in the sense that there is no current reason for the emotions. The outbursts are actually "phantoms" of the original traumas.

Step 5. You may use crutches for a while. If the soul part took away the ability to memorize, for example, you may all of a sudden resort to the crutch of making lists and asking others to remind you of important appointments. This would not have been the pattern prior to the trauma.

Step 6. You are given a prosthetic foot along with extensive instruction on how to use it. However, even if you become adept at it and it looks natural to others, you always know it is not real. You cannot actually feel the foot touching the floor. With the natural trait gone, you can receive extensive help and actually learn how to behave in a way that looks natural to others. But it always feels forced, labored or unnatural to you. For example, if soul loss makes you feel wary around people, you may learn how to act cordial and outgoing. Yet, inside you always feel that shivery shyness. No amount of psychotherapy or instruction makes a dent in it. That is because the part of the soul that would help you feel comfortable is not home!

Soul Retrieval

Step 7. The doctor takes the foot out of the freezer, cleanses it and sutures it back onto your ankle. He has to make sure the bones, tendons, muscles and nerve endings are matched. Then he gives you important advice on how to care for the wound until the next office visit. The shamanic practitioner finds the soul part in the spiritual dimensions, asks for spiritual healing and brings it back to the physical dimension. She blows it into you in a manner that connects it to your being and seals it in with the sound of a shamanic rattle. She then tells you pertinent information about the soul part and your primary issue, and gives you advice on how to work with the soul part until you return for integration and transformation work.

Soul Transformation

Step 8. Despite sterilization of the foot prior to it being reattached, healing still needs to occur between it and your body. During the soul retrieval itself, Spirit heals the soul part so that it does not bring back emotional pain that would make your life worse than before. Even so, a major part of the process afterwards involves coordination between you and the soul part. For this you need to be attentive to your soul part and its needs, and to go inward to integrate it more fully into all parts of you, not just through the emotions and feelings.

Step 9. You are instructed to come back to the doctor for regular check-ups, until full healing occurs. The doctor inspects the wound, to be sure no infection sets in. He also gives you medication to use at home, as needed. The shamanic practitioner asks you to return for facilitated transformation work, to be sure the soul part is fully healed and to help you learn how to use its new aspect of spiritual qualities in a healthy way. She gives you instruction about how to work with it in your daily life.

Step 10a. Star Trek's sci-fi medical technology can heal a broken bone in minutes, whereas our modern medicine requires weeks and months to do the same mending. Healing the soul part through facilitated journeying or trance sessions, using methods in this book, is as rapid as "Star Trek's" medical healing. Full healing, including sweeping away fears, can occur within one or several sessions. Talk therapy, meditation and "mindfulness" methods are slow, like our modern medicine is; they take months or years to achieve healing, if at all.

POSSIBLE CHOICE AFTERMATH #1:
Integration Without Transformation Is The Painful Path.

The following metaphor illustrates what happens if you choose the slow route with your soul part, or choose to abort the process.

Step 10b. If you walk on the foot before it is healed, all the careful matching could be subverted. In that event, there may be pain as well. If you consider the soul part to be completely integrated, yet still experience detriment from your soul retrieval issue and ignore the soul part's pleas for attention, you will sabotage the benefits of the retrieval. You will not have ready access to its strengths. The pain from such undermining often comes across as fear or a sense of wanting to stay away from the supposed external cause of the fear, even though such aversion is misguided. You may be carrying distorted beliefs.

Step 11. If the foot being attached is the size of a three-year-old's and the leg is the size of a forty-year-old's, considerable acceleration of growth as well as of healing is required for a complete match to occur. The young soul part has to get used to the new body, gain access to your life experiences and grow up to your age. If you are open to change, you will allow the strengths of the returned part to be fully effective. Both of you must be willing to give to the other. If it is scary to face the new and heal the old, you will find that facilitated transformation sessions are the gentler, safer, quicker route to healing; then healing occurs in minutes. Trying to run from the fear only magnifies it and slows down your healing.

Step 12. If you fail to return for check-ups and also do not treat the wound with care, including not using medication, the foot could get infected, gangrened and/or shift off line from the bone. You would no longer have practical use of it. If you fail to return for facilitated healing sessions and also do not do inner work with the soul part at home, one of the following could happen:

The worst-case scenario is that the soul part decides to leave again or you deliberately send it away. When a soul part leaves it not only removes its aspect of a spiritual quality, it also leaves behind a lasting impression of emotional pain that cannot be healed. Such action is as emotionally painful as infection and gangrene are physically painful. It is *not* a recommended solution to hardship during the integration process!

A lesser-case scenario, but equally debilitating, is that the soul part "goes underground", i.e., becomes repressed. When this happens, you do not have access to the strengths and qualities that the returned soul part could give you. All you have access to are the distorted attitudes or beliefs that arise from the fear of using your newly returned qualities. This can cause inner turmoil and further relationship problems.

Step 13. The bone connecting the foot to the ankle has to heal. If the foot is in complete alignment with the ankle and it remains so, then the healing is beneficial. If, however, it goes off center, the muscles and tendons may not be able to work the foot correctly and/or the bone has to be re-broken and realigned. The bone, in metaphorical terms, relates to belief systems about self and life, not about religious beliefs; your healing process may require a change of beliefs. The muscles and tendons compare to habits of action; your healing process may require changing habit patterns.

If you choose the long, slow, outer-directed healing route, then the process is very painful, or at the very least, uneventful and unrewarding. "Centering" means going inside self, and the inner-directed way; "Going off center," in the analogy, refers to the outer-directed route. This latter brings emotional turmoil, projection, and trying to "fix" others and current situations. The true fixing, i.e., changing, needs to be within self. Your inner turmoil creates outer havoc. *If* you heal, it may take years to do so.

POSSIBLE CHOICE ALTERNATIVE #2
Fast Transformation Produces Beneficial, Permanent Results.

Step 11. If the foot being attached is the size of a three-year-old's and the leg is the size of a forty-year-old's, considerable acceleration of growth as well as healing is required for a complete match to occur. As said previously, your young soul part has to get used to the new body, gain access to your life experiences and grow up to your age. You need to be open to change, in order to allow the soul qualities of the returned soul part to be fully effective; both of you must be willing to give to each other. A very gentle, safe, quick route to doing this healing is through facilitated-trance Transformation sessions. If you are able to do shamanic journeying or trance on your own, such accelerates the healing even more.

Step 12. You return for check-ups and treat the wound with care, including using medication. The foot does not get infected. You come in for facilitated healing sessions and also do inner work with the soul part at home. You heal any distorted attitudes or beliefs that may arise from the soul loss causes and from fear of using the soul qualities; therefore you have access to the strengths and qualities that the returned soul part carries. There is no danger of the soul part deciding to leave again nor do you want to send it away.

Step 13. The bone connecting the foot to the ankle has to heal. If the foot is in complete alignment with the ankle and remains so, the healing is beneficial. The bone, in soul terms, relates to belief systems about you and life, not religious beliefs.

The Transformed Soul: A Metaphor

Your healing process may require a change of beliefs. The muscles and tendons compare to habits of thought and action; your healing process may require changing habit patterns. During facilitated-journey or trance transformation sessions, these changes happen quickly and painlessly, just as with "Star Trek's" healing technology. Done soon after the retrieval, both you and your soul part have the enthusiasm to help.

Step 14. When fully healed, your foot not only looks and operates naturally, it feels natural! Such is the objective of the healing work. When the soul part is fully healed and transformed, your beliefs, attitudes and habit patterns are in alignment. You not only look and behave naturally, you *feel* natural! Naturalness and wholeness are the objective of this process.

CHAPTER 3

SOUL LOSS

Soul Loss? Can The Soul Be Split?

The soul is that essence given to us by Spirit, our Divine Creator, that is totally unique. No one else's essence can take the place of it, and we cannot remain embodied without it. Religious texts advocate that humans are created in the image of Spirit. "As above so below" is another way of saying that. This means that whatever we see within ourselves is also in Spirit, and whatever we see in the macrocosm of the universe is also within the microcosm of ourselves. Cosmology teaches that Spirit split itself into many sparks so that it could experience its creation more deeply. We are those sparks of Spirit, and the spark resides within the core of our being. If Spirit can divide itself, then can we not do the same?

Perhaps we have just forgotten that we are part of Spirit. Here on Earth we feel separate from each other. We can be intimately connected with people, then go our own separate ways. We die when our soul chooses such, and not when everyone else on the planet dies. The deceased person may not be with us physically, but he or she can be with us in spirit, in our hearts, prayers and dreams.

All of this is the macrocosmic, all-encompassing way of viewing Oneness versus Separation. If that can happen at the macrocosmic level of Spirit, why can it not also occur at the microcosmic level of the individual? "As it is above so is it mirrored below." Said in a microcosmic way: we can lose hair, blood, a limb, and still feel ourselves whole within the incomplete body. Then why can we not maintain a complete body while losing part of our soul? "As below so above."

Numerous world religions say we humans were made in the image of Spirit, thus holograms of it. Think of the difference between a hologram and a snapshot. If we cut a snapshot into quarters then reproduce one quarter of it, we still get a whole picture of just the quarter. On the other hand, if we cut a hologram into quarters and shine a laser beam through one quarter of it, the resulting picture is an exact duplicate of the original *whole* hologram! We cannot tell the difference between the original and the copy.

Each of us feels distinctly individual, i.e., a separate person from others around us. Yet we are also part of this planet, universe, and Spirit. We do not think of ourselves as being just a copy. We are real and whole in our own right.

It is the same experience with our soul parts.

When I talk with a person's soul part during a soul retrieval, it often communicates the feeling that it is a total person within itself. Some are even surprised that there is "someone else" who has the same identity as they, not realizing that they had separated from the body. When a soul part returns to the physical body, at first it continues to see itself as separate, although it may be inside an older larger self. Until it is fully integrated, it also talks with the person as if both are separate.

> *There is a hologram (soul part)*
> *Inside a larger hologram (self)*
> *Of the original picture (Spirit)*

Spiritual Qualities

The soul carries intelligence and the ability to use various spiritual qualities that are our divine birthright. Each spiritual quality has a unique feel to it. We acknowledge that truth when we say "I am loving" or "I am truthful" or "I am compassionate" or "I am decisive." At those moments, a specific spiritual quality takes over our full awareness. That quality is used and protected by a specific part of the soul; only that part of the soul knows how to effectively and fully use it in an innate way. For example, Decisiveness cannot do the Loving job, any more than the stomach can do the heart's job. However, the two can work cooperatively with each other. That is what helps make us whole, well-rounded individuals.

A partial list of these spiritual qualities is as follows:

Hope	Trust	Caring
Centering	Wisdom	Empathy
Truth	Vision	Magnetism
Spirituality	Love	Tenderness
Innocence	Compassion	Charisma
Faith	Appreciation	Generosity

Soul Loss

Magnetism	Self-love	Perseverance
Enthusiasm	Strength	Courage
Passion	Focus	Responsibility
Spontaneity	Self-reliance	Stamina
Playfulness	Decisiveness	Power
Creativity	Spiritual will	Authority
Sensitivity	Togetherness	Right timing
Psychism	Morality	Practicality
Perceptivity		Memorization
Joy	Tenacity	
Self-esteem	Resilience	
Memory	Sense of purpose	Set boundaries
Concentration	Know who you are	Emotional resilience
Gracefulness	Self-appreciation	See whole picture
Belief in self	Stand up for self	Connect heart-head
Body appreciation		Stick-to-itiveness

Kabalah (Hebrew and Christian mysticism) says that we have many points of consciousness throughout our whole being. Memory and thinking are not just in the brain, but also throughout the body and aura. We can put our whole awareness into the hand or the heart or the leg. We can think with the heart and love with the head. We have many parts within the whole of self, both physically and personally.

Think of the various figures of speech we use. For instance, if we are trying to decide where to go on vacation, we may say: "Part of me likes the beauty of Alaska. Part of me desires the warmth of the Caribbean. Another part of me is intrigued with the history of Rome." The words imply an inner conflict with aspects of self: appreciation of beauty, enjoyment of creature comforts, and mental curiosity.

Why Soul Loss?

When we go through emotional or physical trauma, loss of a loved one, neglect, or needing to adapt to a long-standing difficult situation, we may tend to go momentarily out of body. This is a coping mechanism that helps us avoid the full impact of the pain. This planet is a laboratory for learning and spiritual growth. It is not intended that any of us self-destruct here. To ensure this, we are given a way out, a way to partially leave a life that feels too hard to withstand. *It also is not Spirit's intention that we obliterate, for all eternity, any divinely ordained spiritual qualities and soul parts.* If a life experience threatens the survival of a spiritual quality, Spirit allows angels to step in and offer us the option to leave. The soul part carrying the endangered quality is the part that chooses to go. It does this because it cares so deeply about preserving that trait, or it is so concerned about *our* survival, that it chooses to remove its quality in order to soften our load.

For instance, if a child stands up for himself against his parents, he is spanked. The parents perceive this quality as rebelliousness rather than the spiritual strength it actually is. The more he objects, the worse the spanking gets. Finally, the soul part that carries the "standing up for self" quality decides to leave, in order for the child to get along more harmoniously within the family.

None of us is given more nor less than we can handle, at the *spiritual* level. Sure, at times it feels like we are on overload or about to go over the brink. But, until we "cry uncle" or until Spirit intervenes, we may find that our pain continues to escalate, or we encounter an unexpected inner/outer resource that helps gets us through tough times. One of these resources is soul loss. As I have learned in my training and have witnessed in my experience as a shamanic practitioner, there is also a lesson to be learned when soul loss happens. **When soul parts leave, they are not allowed to return on their own.** Why would they want to return to a situation they deem untenable?! They also are not allowed to communicate with us nor influence us in any manner. That may seem like a pretty heavy lesson, but it is actually a kindness that Spirit bestows. Any contact with the soul part would only re-traumatize us, that is, remind us of the situation that made it leave and revive painful emotions. If it was difficult for the soul part it was also difficult for the rest of us who stayed in body.

Another factor in soul loss is that it helps us stay alive and at the same time cope with life's trials. If soul parts could not split off, our alternative would be to die. Premature dying would thwart our learning process, mission in life and Spirit's purpose for this life.

Sometimes soul loss is purely a learning mechanism. A soul part may have Spirit's permission to leave voluntarily so that the rest of the ensouled body can learn a valuable spiritual lesson. By "lesson" I do not mean punishment. A hypothetical example of this is: A little girl's spiritual purpose in this lifetime is to learn how to relate empathically with others. A sense of impenetrable boundaries would inhibit this learning. Therefore, the part of her soul that carries the "boundaries" quality decides to remove some of it by going into soul loss. The hole in her boundaries enables her to feel others' feelings and to be influenced by them. When she firmly learns empathy, Spirit returns the soul part, who can then help her use the strengths of strong, impenetrable boundaries.

The following is a demonstration of a soul part's voluntary departure:

> **CASE STUDY** *of Paula.* Here is a segment of one of Paula's soul retrieval transformation sessions. During this session, I interact with both Paula and her soul part named "Ten." We call her "Ten" because that was the age the soul loss occurred.
>
> During a shamanic journey, "Ten" sits in front of Paula and does not speak. She is poised and serene.
> *Maryphyllis:* Paula, does age Ten have any messages for you?
> *Ten (through Paula):* There is more to learn about the ways of women. Paula is moving into a new stage of being a woman. I will help her use and gain that knowledge. I bring women's wisdom.
> *Maryphyllis:* Paula, does Ten want to share why she left?
> *Ten:* I left because it was inappropriate for me to have all this knowledge then. My family could not handle deep wisdom from such a young child as I was.

What Is Soul Loss?

When part of us recedes totally into spiritual realms, it cuts off all mental and emotional contact with us. Because of the disconnection, we have no way to access its help and communication. This is called "soul loss". We suffer the loss of part of our soul, but soul *loss* does not mean forever. It is "misplaced" only, i.e., not in contact with the rest of the soul in body.

I once had a dream that clearly describes the soul loss process: I saw a three-dimensional form of myself as seen by Spirit. A multitude of little specks of light, resembling newsprint dots, surrounded and pervaded my form. Specks comprising my physical body were densely packed; those in the aura around my body became increasingly more sparse the farther they extended away from the physical. As I watched, a slim column of the specks of light lifted upwards away from the left side of my aura, first hovering a little above my head and finally disappearing high up into the spiritual dimensions. The column left a gap in the aura near my body.

The dream illustrates how a portion of the soul retreats: first it contemplates whether or not to leave. When it fully decides to go, it recedes completely into spiritual dimensions, leaving a hole in our being and capacities. Clairvoyants say they have seen holes in people's auras. My dream showed that holes indicate where in the body or aura the soul loss occurred. The holes do not necessarily divulge the circumstances that caused the loss.

In the dream, the soul portion stayed close to my body, hovering near but not in my thought realm. She could watch the rest of me in body but could not participate in my deliberations and activities. She could only wait until such time as I could call her back. Any impulse to return was thwarted by a subtle energy that gently kept her at bay. Although she resided only in my spiritual level and could not communicate with me, my soul part still carried a sense of "me-ness", i.e., the memories, feelings and thoughts were "mine."

The Soul Part's Experience While Gone

The moment a soul part leaves, its growth is arrested. It stays at the age, mindset and state of emotions it was in at the moment it left. It cannot benefit from any experience or growth we attain. It is totally absorbed in its feelings and like an endless loop it obsesses over the soul loss causes. Usually it does not wonder if our life is now better or easier to cope with because it is unaware of how much time has gone by since it left. Some soul parts actually do not even know they are gone!

If a soul part leaves due to a traumatic circumstance, its obsessing is clouded with feelings of despair, fear, anger, hopelessness, or shock. If a child is tightly controlled by his family, the soul part may leave in order to indulge in play, creativity, freedom, or love of all life. If it leaves the body before that trait is tainted by negative emotions, its obsessing is joyful and uplifting. If a soul part leaves for a spiritual purpose, then its obsessing is definitely uplifting. There is only bright vibrancy, without negativity.

Causes for soul loss are as varied and individual as we are. An incident that creates soul loss for one person does not do so for another.

Symptoms Of Impending Soul Loss.
 If any of the following symptoms apply to your experience, part of your soul is seriously considering leaving:
 • Feeling unappreciated, even though people express appreciation of you.
 • Feeling that no matter what you do, your efforts are thwarted, even though intellectually you see success in your life.
 • Feeling like you want to move away from your town, in hopes that things will be better elsewhere. Yet, you intellectually realize that things are alright, here.
 • Sudden onset of depression, accompanied by any or all of the above three symptoms.
 • Feeling you want to die, accompanied by any or all of the above symptoms. *This last one is a major "red flag" that soul loss is* **imminent**. *It is vital to* **get help at once!**
 Notice that in each of the above symptoms there is an intellectual awareness that contradicts the feeling-generated thoughts. The intellectual aspect is coming from the part of you that is ok with how you are viewing and interacting with life. The feelings-generated thoughts are coming from a part of your soul who despairs that its prized spiritual quality is being squelched.
 This conflict needs to be looked at with utmost seriousness. As soon as possible, you should confer with your spirit helpers and the soul part that carries the quality in question, to find a way to work with that quality without negating it. Your spiritual qualities are bestowed on you by Spirit. Spirit intends that you use all of them with respect, reverence, and in balance with each other.

Where Does It Go?
 A soul part may go anywhere in the spiritual dimensions adjacent to this physical world. By going there, it cuts off all contact with mental, emotional and physical levels of our being. Usually they do not watch us nor are they aware of our activities. It is totally isolated the whole time it is away.
 Some soul parts stay at the physical site where trauma occurred. Some stay close to their physical body. They can watch, but are powerless to intervene and interact with us. These parts often say, "I've been near you, watching you all this time, anxiously waiting to come back."

Some are attached to other people. This is the result of "soul stealing" when other people take them, in an effort to control us. It is called "soul giving" when we give pieces of our soul to others, out of love, rage, fear or trying to control them. Whether we verbalize it as "trying to control others," or "giving them my heart", it is still soul loss.

Giving and stealing soul parts is a common occurrence in society. Unfortunately, it always leads to strife and someone feeling less able. Others' soul parts do not help us. Their energy only weighs us down and projects negative thoughts and attitudes into our minds every hour of the day. They can even counteract any actions we wish to take and attitudes we want to have about self, others and life. This inner conflict produces more and more negativity within us. Soul stealing and soul giving result in increased anger, strife, control, reprisal, being out of control, inciting problems with loved ones, loss of soul parts, loss of energy, loss of sleep, lack of peace, fighting, and more. If we think and act hatefully toward the person who owns the soul parts we are carrying, we may become abusive or allow ourselves to be abused. This in turn increases our inner sense of guilt, fear and low self-worth. It is a cycle that forever spirals downward. Carrying others' soul parts causes inner conflict and increased friction in our relationships.

If we literally give parts of our soul to loved ones, with the mistaken intent of helping them, we actually create the opposite affect. The soul parts *hinder* our loved ones from learning how to be self-supporting; they may feel resentful or develop a sense of powerlessness to act on their own behalf. At the same time, we feel a drain of energy and growing ineptness in our ability to help. Hard feelings build between us.

If we fling emotional energy and soul parts to another person when "lashing out" emotionally, we deplete our energy. We solve nothing. The other person's animosity toward us increases because our soul parts constantly "yammer" in their mind. An excellent illustration of this is the story of my client Rosalee.

CASE STUDY *of Rosalee.* During a soul transformation session, Rosalee did a shamanic journey to her twelve-year-old soul part. It brought to her awareness the memory of an *inner* incident which Rosalee did not recall ever having in physical life nor prior to the soul retrieval. In the memory, she was standing in her school's hallway, motionless, while her friend Milly shouted at her constantly. Milly told her she was "bad, a no-good worthless person and would rot in hell for what she did!" At the same time, Rosalee contradicted this by saying to herself current day truths such as, "I am creatively talented, a top scholar, and am successful in my work. I have close friends and have always been spiritually motivated."

After Rosalee and I worked with this self-belief she noticed a difference in the hall scene. She saw *three* images of her friend all at the same time! I realized that Milly had angrily flung several of her soul parts at Rosalee. These soul parts were a major cause of Rosalee's low opinion of herself. Every time Rosalee thought well of herself, Milly's soul parts contradicted her. It was a continual battle every hour of every day, and had been for decades.

Signs Of Others' Soul Parts On You
• You over-react to the other person's actions or words.
• The other person "pushes your buttons" easily.
• You daydream about arguing with that person.
• Anxiety feelings when they first come to you. It is a feeling of having more energy than you know what to do with.
• Feeling an inner contradiction to wanting to take action.

Signs Of Others' Stealing Your Soul Parts
• Feeling irresistibly drawn to another person although your rational mind declares there is no compatibility. You just do not want to be there.
• Feeling drained of energy after intense emotional expression with someone. This also can manifest as becoming very sleepy.
• Feeling drained of energy when near the person or when you have thoughts of them.
• The last two are a *BIG SIGNAL* that the stealing is going on *right now*.

What To Do About Soul Stealing?
There are immediate remedies if you feel that soul stealing is happening to you right now.

An energy drain indicates someone is stealing from you; in some circles, this is called "psychic vampirism." The person may or may not be aware of it; do not place blame. Instead, focus on your own energy, affirm "this is *mine!*" and envision it coming back to you. If the drain seems more than you can handle, call on

Spirit to help you and at the same time use every ounce of mental and spiritual energy you have. You can also command your subconscious to bring your own energy back into you. When your soul energy returns to you, you will feel *instantly* more alive and energetic.

If you feel an excess of energy, energetic anxiety and/or notice others around you becoming depleted or drowsy, you may be stealing their energy. Do not place blame on yourself. Instead, focus on your own energy, affirm, "this is mine and I release yours" and let go. If you feel you may lose some of your soul in the process, focus on Spirit and trust that your soul essence will stay with you. It will. When the other person's energy is released, you will feel more calm and peaceful. Others around you will look more alert and awake.

In both of the immediately previous instances, forgiveness is a very important aid and component.

Important note: The above advice is for soul-stealing-in-progress. These methods do not work for reclaiming or returning soul parts that have been missing for a while. Those require training in how to do soul retrievals.

Memory Loss

When the soul parts leave, they may take with them all or part of the memories concerning the event that propels them into soul loss. As a result, we are not able to have enough recall to consider the incident important, much less do therapy on it. When the soul part returns, it can also return these memories to us. It is then that we realize profoundly the immense significance of the event.

At the time of the soul retrieval, many people recognize instantly the circumstances described to them as to why and at what age the soul part left. This is because the causal incidents carry intense emotions and are memorable. Yet others are surprised that a soul part would leave for a seemingly insignificant reason. Some of the subtleties I have heard include having to leave Grandma after a wonderful visit, or a close older sister starting first grade, or a gentle word of disapproval from Mom. In such cases, people often comment, "If I had had the best therapy in the world and had worked for tens of years, I would never have guessed that this incident would have caused soul loss!"

The above are more subtle reasons why Spirit allows parts of us to go into soul loss. More dramatic and pervasive causes of soul loss are described below.

Symptoms Of Soul Loss

Each of the following symptoms may indicate that a soul part has left. The more that apply, the more sure it is that there has been soul loss. Keep in mind, however, that symptoms may also indicate some other cause, such as physical ills or discarnate beings attached to you. If this seems to be the case, consider seeking healing work on simultaneous levels, such as, retrieval *and* seeing your M.D., or retrieval *and* getting energy work.

Note: the double bullets (• •) indicate symptoms that are true of *all* soul loss, regardless of cause.

• • *Fear* is a general symptom of *all* soul loss, just as pain is a symptom of something being wrong within the physical body. *Unreasoning fears* are fears that do not seem to have a point of origin. They are pervasive and ever-present. They may throw you into an unwilling "trance," setting aside rational thinking; your fears, rather than your thoughts, control you. As each soul part returns, it wipes away more of your fear. When all of the soul parts are back, unreasoning fear leaves permanently. You will still have the protective influence of natural caution and the kind of fear that serves to warn you of true danger. This kind of fear works in balance with rational thinking. It does not linger for long periods of time; rather, it leaves when the danger is over.

• *Unexplainable emotional outbursts* are "phantom residuals" of the soul loss cause, just as phantom sensations occur with an amputated limb from the physical body.

• • *Loss of vitality* or a sense that some of the light or color has gone out of life. Returned soul parts add more vitality, energy, color and depth of connection to life.

• • *Feeling empty, fragmented, not quite whole.* It is a sense that something is missing within *you,* not just in your life. This is a general symptom of soul loss creating holes in the aura. Returned soul parts automatically help you feel more whole and complete.

• *Feeling like you are sleepwalking* through life, that is, semi-conscious. With each soul part that returns, you feel increasingly more present and alert, in a relaxed way. When all of the soul is back in body, you feel totally present in life.

- **_Feeling alienated from life_** and the planet; feeling like you are an unwilling observer who never fits in. With your soul in body, you feel connected to life and very much part of this planet. Even if your ways are different from others around you, you still feel like you fit in. That is because _you_ are now fitting in with your _self._
- • **_Difficulty concentrating or uncontrolled day-dreaming or dissociation._** You try to focus, but your mind keeps drifting away to other things, or you simply "space-out". This is especially significant if it applies to circumstances in which you are genuinely interested. Your subconscious mind is unsuccessfully trying to reach information it knew you once had. When the soul parts are back, the subconscious can find the desired information without sending the mind drifting.
- **_Emotional numbness._** You cannot feel sorrow, joy, excitement, nor other emotions. You might be able to _act_ emotionally, but you cannot feel it. When the soul is fully embodied and the soul loss causes are healed, emotional aliveness in balance with rational thinking is a natural state.
- **_Grief_** that will not heal, going on for years unabated. Natural grief lessens over time. If it does not, you may be grieving not just for the loss of a loved one, but also for a lost soul part. When the soul part returns, the grief miraculously leaves.
- **_Depression._** There are numerous causes of depression, thus there is no _one_ way for everyone to heal it. Causes include soul loss, grief, chemical imbalance, food or substance allergy, negative thinking, low self-esteem, repressed anger, inability or refusal to approach Spirit, not following Spirit's design for your life. Depression that also includes one of the other symptoms on this list says more strongly that soul loss may be the cause of it. That is particularly true if there is a grief component to the depression; you may be depressed and grieving for the loss of part of your soul.

Returned soul parts can immediately alleviate depression that is caused by grieving over a lost soul part, inability to approach Spirit, or not following Spirit's design for your life. To heal other causes of depression, you may need repeated soul retrievals (low self-esteem, especially), or to work simultaneously with soul retrieval and another form of therapy, or strictly with a different form of therapy.

• **_Depression that feels suicidal or hopeless,_** accompanied by feeling less whole and missing an ability you used to have, is a _strong_ indication of soul loss. _It might also be an indication of impending soul loss._

• **_Hopelessness_** nearly always accompanies soul loss that occurred due to long-standing neglect or traumatic conditions. At some point in the soul retrieval process you should ask for the return of "Hope", which is a specific spiritual quality. Full healing of the soul-loss-causes and transformation of returned soul parts is important for allowing "Hope" to be back permanently.

• **_Noticeably different_** after a trauma, i.e., noticeably less; perhaps missing a quality or ability that you had prior to the trauma. Examples: feeling less like yourself; feeling less whole afterwards; self-expression is difficult afterwards; some form of learning is no longer as easy as it used to be. Return of soul parts naturally creates more wholeness, helps you feel more like yourself, recaptures the ability you knew you had, and helps you express yourself.

• **_Resistance to taking action_** in an area that used to be easy prior to the soul loss event. You can think about taking action, but you cannot summon the will to do so. For example: it may be more difficult to be compassionate now, or it takes more effort to be decisive, or you really want to write that story but just cannot get started, or organizing is now so alien that it is simply out of the question.

When the soul parts return, you find it easy to take action on your thoughts. You think about wanting to do something and suddenly find yourself doing it naturally. You do not have to force yourself to act.

• **_Missing a spiritual quality_** all humans are supposed to have. You may feel like you have to force a specific quality, because it does not feel natural. Forcing the quality may be accompanied by a sense of being egotistical or lacking self-confidence. Such symptoms signify that the soul part took some of that quality when it left. Returned soul parts and their spiritual qualities give you a sense of naturalness to your expression. There is less egotism and more self-confidence because you have more aspects of the qualities at your disposal.

• **_Years of trying to improve_** in a specific area, yet always coming up against a block. There is little to no improvement. Just as you have to attend a lesson in order to be taught, so you have to be in the body in order to change and grow. You cannot develop that specific trait if the soul part that carries it is not home. To try to do so would be as futile as expecting an orchestra to sound complete without its violins.

When the soul parts return, you have the resources you need in order to make the changes you desire. The changes occur much more easily and quickly.

• *Easily swayed* by others' emotions, to the point of acting out *their* feelings and not your own. The holes in your aura allow external influence, including emotional energy from living people. Returned soul parts fill in those holes and create a natural buffer that allows you to think for yourself and not be unduly influenced by other people's feelings.

• *"Hanging on by a thread"*. Major stress of feeling like you are "hanging on by a thread", that if you let go, you will fade away. This, when combined with other symptoms on this list, can indicate major soul loss. *It can also indicate that you are missing the etheric webbing that holds all the soul parts together.* Returned soul parts can help you feel more together, more relaxed, less tenuous about life. With most or all of the soul embodied, there is none of this kind of stress. You may have stress related to life circumstances, maybe, but not the kind of stress that tries to hold the *self* together.

• *Addictions.* Does it feel like you are trying to fill up a hole in yourself through eating, drugs, alcohol, or sex? But the void is always there, never satisfied? Or does it feel like there is an outside force impelling you into the addictive behavior? There may be layers of factors at work in the addiction, or only one cause of it: soul loss, karmic lesson, discarnate entity attachment, genetic predisposition, or chemical imbalance.

For full healing, you may have to work on several levels at once, such as, energy work *and* soul retrieval, psychotherapy *and* soul retrieval, and so on. When the holes in your being are filled by returned and transformed soul parts you may no longer feel the need to fill your body with an addictive substance.

• *History of abuse, trauma or neglect* in and of itself may not necessarily assure that there has been soul loss. What is too much for one person to handle is a "piece of cake" for someone else. However, if a history of abuse, trauma or neglect accompanies any of the other symptoms in this list, it is quite likely you have suffered soul loss. Soul retrieval, integration and transformation are an excellent tool for recovery from *Post*

Traumatic Stress Syndrome, which often accompanies having endured abuse and trauma.

• *Symptoms of spirit possession.* Spirit possession means that discarnate spirits, i.e., deceased persons, attach to a living human's aura rather than going on to the Light. This can occur because the human has had soul loss, thus creating a "hole" in the aura. Discarnates also can at times force soul loss. If there are discarnates attached, you need to have these removed by someone who knows what they are doing; do not try it on your own. You also probably need soul retrievals to fill up the spaces so that other discarnates can not attach.

• *Symptoms of major dissociative disorder.* Dissociation itself is a major symptom of soul loss. Soul retrieval can help in some instances. If you have been diagnosed as having a major mental illness and want soul retrievals, you should work simultaneously with your psychiatrist's or psychotherapist's supervision.

Soul Loss Versus Other Maladies

• *Dissociation.* Psychologists say that dissociation manifests as "spacing-out," spontaneous daydreaming, or inability to concentrate. They consider it to be an observable phenomenon that is an ongoing problem rather than occasional, as occurs in less severe cases of soul loss that this book tends to address.

When dissociation happens it is a signal that there probably has been soul loss in your past. With soul loss, the mind is trying to access information or a soul quality that is no longer there. A metaphor of this may be that of reaching for the support of a sturdy fence, finding only a hole and falling through. In dissociation, you mentally reach for a desired quality or memory, find a blank, and momentarily fall out of the body. It feels like inadvertent daydreaming or attention wandering.

Dissociation's effect depends upon the frequency and degree that it occurs in your life. If you experience constant dissociation you may qualify for major mental illness due to being out of touch with reality. But this is not typical of most people. In fact, you can be fully functional in society, hold down a job, have good relationships, and still have suffered soul loss...which probably accounts for the majority of the world's population.

• *Dissociative Identity Disorder (DID), formerly known as Multiple Personality Disorder.* On the surface, this disorder may sound like soul loss and soul retrieval, but it is not the same.

In *DID*, the alters (different personalities) can appear, leave and appear again, over and over at will. With soul loss, the soul parts that leave cannot return on their own. It takes active intervention by a skilled shamanic practitioner, or an act of spiritual grace, for a soul part to be brought back.

With *DID*, greater wholeness is *not* the norm. There is usually amnesia of other alters, plus feelings of fragmentation. With soul retrieval, wholeness *is* the norm, and we gain recall of more memories without the loss of any.

Although these two are not the same, massive soul loss creates psychic holes that can allow *DID* to occur.

• *Spirit Possession.* Many of the symptoms of soul loss and spirit possession overlap (see the previous heading). That is no coincidence. Soul loss creates holes in the aura that leave us open to outside influence. Minor outside influence manifests as being gullible, easily swayed by other people, or wanting other people to make decisions for you. In major outside influence, the holes can leave you open to illness or to attachment by discarnate spirits. However, not all spirit possession is preceded by soul loss and not all soul loss leads to spirit possession

• *Memory Loss.* Some people report inability to remember their childhood and wonder if that is due to soul loss. It is true that soul parts can take away all or part of the memories concerning the incident that made them leave. However, soul loss is not the only cause of memory loss. If it were, you who do not recall your childhood would be in either a coma or a mental hospital with severe mental illness because you would also be missing a lot of spiritual qualities related to everyday skills and language. Obviously, this is not the case. You are functional in society. The fact that you have skills, talents, focusing ability, and recall of everyday information indicates that there is selective memory and repression going on. You may have given your subconscious the command to not bring specific types of memories to mind. Your childhood memory loss may well be due to selective repression.

However, massive memory loss is an indication that something painful happened. Soul retrieval can help heal and alleviate that pain as well as restore some of the memories, if you wish such to occur.

The Shadow

In today's world, soul loss is creating more and more soul loss, with little awareness that it is possible to bring soul parts back. The original virtuous intent is fast becoming a fault. Fragmentation is escalating pain and problems for the planet and us. We are not operating "on all cylinders," so to speak. (I wonder if wars and power struggles originate from soul loss? Whole people love and feel kinship with all of life; fighting is not an option with them.)

The reason why we feel less capable, less whole and less alive after soul loss is because we are missing the benefit of spiritual qualities, memories and our unique spiritual essence called the soul. We cannot access it because the pathway for doing so has been severed. We adapt to being "less." Because our memory of the soul part's trait is incomplete, we adopt dysfunctional beliefs, attitudes and patterns. Trying to imitate the soul part's quality would be like trying to imitate a family member. We can approximate part of their actions, but we don't have sufficient inner knowledge of who they are to be able to imitate them in *all* situations. Likewise, others of our soul parts can take over some of the functions of a missing soul part but it can't duplicate all of them. The correct soul part has to be in body in order for us to act in a fully functional manner.

Famed psychologist Carl Jung defined the "shadow" as unconscious negativity or undeveloped traits that we are unwilling to express. In relation to soul retrieval, the shadow is a part of self that compensates for the loss of a soul part and the spiritual quality it carries. It is as if our subconscious mind says, "I know I once had this quality, but now I cannot find it anywhere within myself. Let's see, what was that like?" And then it conjures up the original as best it can recall. The trouble is, it does not have enough knowledge of all facets of the spiritual quality and the soul part to help us feel natural using it.

For example, my "6M" soul part took a chunk of decisiveness with her when she left. All my life, if a situation were not crystal clear, I would agonize over a decision. I weighed the various viewpoints, made lists to compare, and asked others for their opinions. But the decisive aspect of knowing when to call it quits and just choose was not there. Other people said I was decisive and indeed it may have looked that way to them; but they did not know what I was feeling! A major part of my agonizing process involved fear: fear of making the wrong decision, fear of the results of my decision, fear of how people would react to it, and so on. When I finally made the choice, I carried it out anxiously and vociferously. If it was the wrong one, I went through with it anyway. If anyone commented on it I became either defensive or cowering.

Part of the problem with incomplete memory of the original trait, and trying to recapture the full feeling of it, has to do with the subconscious mind. According to Hawaiian Shamanism, i.e., Huna, the subconscious is the storehouse of all memories and the generator of emotions and feelings. It knows when it does not have all the information necessary to feel completely natural at expressing the missing quality. Even though it knows there is missing information, it still wants desperately to comply with the conscious mind's command to act. Therefore it creates a semblance of the desired action. It also adds feelings of inadequacy, uncertainty, shame, fear, or false bravado. At best, we come across as false, confused, or conveying mixed messages. At worst, we express emotions that are out of proportion to the current event.

The fears listed in my personal illustration of "6M" were generated by my subconscious. It knew there was not enough information available to know when I had reached the correct choice. It would continue to bring more and more choices to mind, asking me (my conscious mind) to make a decision. At the same time, it expressed constant worry and fear that it could not give me all the information I needed. This was the source of my fears around the decision.

An analogy: "Jake" has expert ability at walking with an artificial leg. It may look natural to someone else, but *he* does not feel natural with it. Only the real leg would give the sense of naturalness. If anyone mentions how he walks, he feels insulted and becomes defensive.

So it is with spiritual qualities. We can *act* outgoing, for example, but if we do not feel that inside, it always feels forced – no matter how natural it looks to someone else. If anyone calls attention to it, strong emotions may well up in self-defense.

A metaphor: The whole, complete self is like an egg. Take that egg, pierce small holes into each end of the shell and blow yolk and albumen out of it. You now have an eggshell that *looks* complete but actually is not; it is fragile. Just so, soul loss produces a shell of the spiritual quality. It is without substance and feels unnatural and hollow; others would say we are fragile.

Soul retrieval and transformation returns substance to that shell, making it whole, strong and natural once again.

> ***Soul loss creates shadow.***
> ***The shadow manifests***
> ***as a dysfunctional way of feeling and behaving.***

When the soul part with its spiritual quality returns and is fully transformed, actions feel innate. They no longer have the shadow quality. The returning soul (reality) wipes away the shadow (falsehood). The subconscious is so relieved at finally being able to find all the information it needs, that it exudes joy, delight and naturalness into our feeling nature. It no longer has fear and nervousness about the spiritual quality. It emotes authenticity when we express the quality.

> ***When the soul parts return, the ego traits disappear***
> ***Just as when the light returns, the shadow disappears.***
> ***The soul and its spiritual qualities are the light.***

"All answers and all healing are within us" is a statement made by many spiritual traditions. That is true only if all parts of us are "home" and we are in conscious contact with our spirit helpers. If part of us is missing, we have no recourse but to seek aid from other people. When our totality is home, we have access to all of our inner wisdom. Outer contact then becomes a choice, a preference, rather than a compulsion.

CHAPTER 4

SOUL RETRIEVAL

Soul retrieval has nothing to do with raising the dead or calling deceased people to come talk to us. Rather, it is the process of bringing back to us parts of our soul that left the body. Retrieval helps us feel more whole and alive. The returning parts bring back more memory of the soul loss causal incidents, as well as the talents and strengths that enrich our life.

That is the blessing of soul retrieval:

Re-membering our soul into wholeness,

Re-membering our connection to all life,

Re-membering our divinely ordained soul qualities,

Re-membering our memories.

In a few instances when I was working with clients, my spirit helpers wiped away all the painful memories of the soul part being retrieved because either these memories would have been detrimental to the person, or the person already had the memories and just did not need to be reminded of the trauma. In such instances, the memory absence in no way inhibits the full use of the soul part's spiritual strengths.

Retrieval can happen in spontaneous ways. If you have experienced a dramatic breakthrough either from meditation or in therapy or just plain spontaneously, and your life is forever changed without back-sliding in a week or two, then in all likelihood that experience was a soul retrieval. Spontaneous retrieval seems to occur when the soul parts are near you in this physical dimension, i.e., "middle world", aware of your presence, and Spirit agrees that you are ready for their return. Other soul parts may not be aware of the possibility for retrieval and may also reside out of reach from the physical realm.

Spontaneous retrieval does not happen just because we want it to. Spontaneous, i.e., passive, methods are "catch as catch can," playing the waiting game, so to speak. If anyone says, "Your soul parts are not returning at this time because you are not ready for them," know that is not necessarily so! You may just need a little help from someone who is trained in shamanic soul retrieval, to find and return soul parts that are otherwise inaccessible via passive methods. There is a precedent to this, set by world shamanic cultures. Siberian shamans report that they encourage their people to call back their own soul parts. But if the soul does not return in this way, the shaman travels to the more hidden areas of spiritual dimensions to do a soul retrieval for them.

Do not assume you are not ready for the soul parts if you cannot draw them back on your own.

Spontaneous soul retrievals often bring back soul parts that have left more recently. They come back in response to the work you have already done, and help to finish that segment of healing work. However, they do not necessarily heal the whole issue. The only form of soul retrieval I know of that *actively* seeks and retrieves soul parts is the shamanic form.

Core Soul Parts

Core soul parts are ones that started the soul loss regarding specific issues. Soul parts who leave prior to age five often are connected to a deep-seated belief about self, others, Spirit, and what life is about. These "Core Parts" anchor the soul into the body. If they leave, they open the opportunity for other parts to leave for similar reasons.

For instance, my "6M" soul part took the spiritual qualities "Decisiveness" and "Standing Up For Myself" with her when she left at the age of six months. At later ages, other soul parts left because I could not adequately stand up for myself. If, for example, someone's Self-Love core part leaves, then future soul loss may occur because of not being able to love and respect self.

The difference between retrieving core soul parts and more recent soul parts can be compared to pulling a weed out of the ground. If we take off only the leaves, or cut the plant at ground level, the weed will merely sprout up more of itself. This is analogous to returning more recent soul parts. We may feel an energy boost for a while, but it will not heal the core cause of our issue. As a result, we could continue to have unsolvable problems with the issue unless we can bring back the core cause parts.

If we take the weed out by the roots, the weed does not return. The core parts are the roots of a particular soul loss issue. As they return and are healed, we will not suffer further soul loss for the same issues. They also create a more dramatic improvement in life when fully transformed. In some cases, the healed core part may help retrieve other soul parts that left for the same reason, i.e., spontaneous retrieval.

There are also *core* core parts. These are ones that link with all or nearly all the other soul parts and qualities. In so doing, they strengthen our expression of other spiritual qualities. My 6M is one such *core* core part. She gave me the ability to stand up for myself. Linking with "Unconditional Love" she helped me dare to reach out to others in friendliness. Linking with "Wisdom," she helped me dare to express my wisdom in appropriate circumstances. Linking with "Courage," she helped me get past the habit of just enduring a tough situation, to actually taking action in those scary events.

Spirit determines what soul parts we are ready to handle and transform safely. Sometimes a secondary core part, one that left a little later in age, has to return first in order to prepare us for the true core part. The secondary part had a hand in cementing into us that issue in life that has been so hard to work with. However, Spirit also wants to help us with what we ask. The soul parts that return do this, whether they are core parts, secondary core parts or later ones. When we ask, we receive...in this case, safely.

Our Unique Experiences

Many people feel greater wholeness and completeness just after the soul retrieval. From there, the experience varies, depending upon the spiritual qualities you ask for. You determine what qualities you want retrieved or what wounds you want to heal. Spirit determines what soul parts will best address your request and what you can transform without being overwhelmed.

Each soul retrieval you receive may be different from previous ones. The soul part's style of expression, the nature of the spiritual quality it returns to you and the circumstances that made it leave all determine its effects on you. For example:
- In some retrievals you may feel energy movement within.
- In others, tears may well up.
- In some soul retrievals, it is days before you feel the effects.
- In others, the experience may be uplifting and buoyant from the beginning.
- In some, nothing happens until you start the transformation process.

- In others, the soul parts act positively and naturally right away.

Spiritual qualities are powerful resources for making needed changes in life. In many instances, they cause spontaneous change because it is their role to act decisively and naturally. One of my clients, Maia, described how one of her soul parts influenced her and propelled her into spontaneity.

> *CASE STUDY of Maia.* In 1995 Maia got a soul retrieval to heal her intense fear of speaking in front of groups larger than four people. She had felt this way as far back as she could remember and had tried everything possible to overcome it, to no avail.
> Within a month after her soul retrieval she attended a seminar that enrolled fifteen people. During one discussion she disagreed with what was being said. She went to the chalkboard, drew a diagram and explained her viewpoint to the entire class. When she sat down, she suddenly realized, "Whoa! I never would have done that before the soul retrieval!" What is more, she had felt no fear!
> The soul part and the healing that had taken place gave her the initiative and naturalness to accomplish the previously unthinkable.

Other Forms Of Soul Retrieval
The styles of soul retrieval described thus far in this book are not the only forms available. This section contains descriptions of some other kinds.
• *Soul Parts Appearing Spontaneously in Journeys.* People, who do shamanic journeying faithfully, sometimes report seeing soul parts in the lower world. When left there, they do not grow up. Although you may have communication with them on journeys, you have no communication with them in ordinary reality. Nor do you have access to those soul parts' qualities. All of this indicates that Spirit says they are ready to return to you but are awaiting your conscious permission to do so.
Some talented people have brought these soul parts into their body with good result. Others have not fared well. Be sure you know how to get them fully healed before you welcome them in, so that they give you joy rather than disrupting your life. To learn

how to do this, it may be safer to first obtain a soul retrieval from a qualified shamanic practitioner.

   • *Repression.* Sometimes a soul part does not actually leave the body. Instead, you repress it into a section of the mind that relates to a specific part of the body, such as heart or head. When retrieved, it needs a lot of transformational work, including your personal attention in ordinary reality and extra healing for both you and the soul part in order to avoid falling back into repression.

   • *Soul Retrievals for Animals.* Cats, dogs and other animals respond quite favorably to soul retrieval. One aged dog suddenly started playing with her younger companion animal, something she never would do previously. Another dog stopped his indiscriminate barking and ever after barked only when a stranger entered the property. A very skittish cat became calm and nonchalant after his soul retrieval; not one to express affection toward anyone except his owner, he brushed up against my leg and looked into my eyes as if to say *"thank you!"*

   • *Body Parts.* A soul retrieval for a body part, such as heart or liver, makes us feel more energized, healthy and physically whole. Sometimes a sense of individuality accompanies it and sometimes it does not. The integration work immediately after the retrieval is different from usual soul retrievals. Rest, body focus and little talking are the best ways to start the first day after the retrieval. You may also need a follow-up with your health practitioner regarding any dietary and medical regimens they may have prescribed. You may find it also helpful to discover the spiritual and psychological characteristics of the illness and body part addressed. These give insights on how to work with your health through soul growth. Where the body part also has a sense of individuality connected to it, transformational methods like those in this book are important to carry out.

   CASE STUDY of Hera. In 1995, Hera received a soul retrieval to help her spiritual growth. One of the soul parts said it came back to help heal her allergies to chemicals by making her more resilient. And it did. Prior to the soul retrieval, nothing any health practitioner gave her worked for very long. She could not tolerate a room that had been painted even as long ago as a year or two earlier! Several years after the retrieval, everything her doctors gave her worked. She could tolerate a room that had been painted as recently as a month previously. Hera had to have this soul part back in order for all her other work to take effect. This part was able to hold within her body the beneficial effects any medications and spiritual healings that were given to her.

My Soul Retrieval Process

All soul retrievals are different and all are unique to the person receiving them. However, for the purpose of revealing factors that are important to the transformation process, the following fictionalized description of a soul retrieval is illustrative. It is a generic composite, comprised of a lot of client experiences. It is not intended as a "how to" on soul retrieval nor on shamanic journeying. You will need specific training for those.

Soul Retrieval For "Jan"

Jan came to me for a soul retrieval to heal her low self-esteem. She had been in counseling for years and had felt much improvement. Yet, the self-esteem issue lingered.

The following is an account of Jan's soul retrieval. In order to more profoundly convey the feeling of this experience, I shall describe it in present tense.

As I start on the soul retrieval journey, the first thing I notice is Jan's primary issue. I feel it as if it were mine, and notice metaphorical images that arise: I am reluctant to go to the upper world because of feeling unworthy and ashamed; I also notice a shadow of someone pulling me back, trying to keep me from going up. Knowing that these are feelings from Jan, I summon my will to carry me upwards. As I enter the upper world, I notice that the clouds there are dark; usually they are bright white. I drift up, away from them and my spirit teacher. I cannot hear him and have difficulty maneuvering down to where I can perceive what he is trying to tell me. Again I recognize that these images are metaphors coming from Jan's primary issue, low self-esteem and feeling unworthy, and I summon my spiritual will to bypass them. It is then easier to move closer to my spirit teacher; yet, I feel scared and unworthy...again, Jan's issue.

As I move nearer to my spirit teacher, I notice that Jan's High Self is shining above me and is conveying information to me through my spirit teacher. He says that her low self-esteem is coming from an inability to be close to Spirit. Someone from her childhood was instrumental in closing her down to this aspect of herself. The shadow image that tried to prevent my rise to the upper world was of a man – perhaps her father or her uncle. The dark clouds are a metaphor for feeling unworthy, as well as for emotional despair from childhood. The drifting up away from the dark clouds indicates dissociation and soul loss. My inability, initially, to hear my spirit teacher are a kinesthetic metaphor of her inability to hear her spirit helpers.

Her High Self says also that this is a karmic issue, in regard to her having chosen her family of origin; the problem originated in other lives. He asks me to tell her that Spirit is very pleased with her self-improvement work and that they support her even though she cannot feel it. She has an uncanny ability to be guided to the right healers and modes of help; this guidance is from Spirit.

My spirit teacher says the soul retrieval is needed. It will answer Jan's desire to heal the low self-esteem even though her primary issue is different from what she mentioned. He also says that other forms of healing would not achieve her desired results.

I call for the power animals who help me with soul retrievals, and proceed with my spirit teacher to the area of the upper world where we begin the process. I confer with my spirit teacher to discern which soul parts will best help her heal. We go for the core Soul Parts because she is ready to see the cause that started the whole soul loss process around this issue. There are three soul parts to be retrieved.

My power animals and I traverse the dark skies around to the point in Jan's life where her low self-esteem started. I can feel the pull of it becoming stronger the closer we get to the starting point. I am almost there, when suddenly I feel blocked. I cannot move forward. My power animals direct my attention to a sandstone mountain with a cave entrance. We go in and find a little girl, age five, standing motionless; she wears a dusty blue dress and her head and chest are covered in cobwebs and dust. This metaphorical imagery tells me that the event that caused the soul loss was very traumatic, sending her into catatonic shock and despair.

With special soul retrieval techniques, we bring her out of that area and send her up to the healing angels. They clear away all the pain and negativity she carries, so that Jan will not have to contend with that in addition to what she is already feeling. When this soul part (we call her "five" because that is the age that the trauma occurred) returns from being healed, she appears as old as Jan and her face radiates light. This tells me all her negativity is gone and she will be a strong healing influence for Jan.

*My power animals and I ask her why she left and what
spiritual quality she brings back. She says she left when her uncle
taunted her about girls being worthless. The spiritual quality she
carries is Hope. I ask for no more details than this; the soul part
will give Jan any further information she needs. I ask "five" if she
is willing to return and to help Jan transform. She says yes.*

*As we proceed towards the beginning of Jan's soul loss, we
come across another little girl, also age five, in a flurry of turmoil.
Her head is practically non-existent; all I see are her chest,
clenched fists, a shabby brown dress, and big people crowded
around her. This metaphorical imagery tells me that her
emotions prevailed, there were adults she was fighting against,
and that she felt like "dirt."*

*My power animals put the first soul part in a safe spot and
then help me focus on this second one. We send her to the Light
for healing.*

*When she returns, she is still age five, but now clad in a pink
dress, and her face is flushed. This imagery conveys that healing
occurred and she feels better about her femininity. My power
animals and I ask her why she left and what quality she carries.
She says she was the first to leave during the same incident as the
other age-five soul part. The spiritual quality she carries is a
feeling-connection with Spirit. I ask her if she is willing to return
and to help Jan transform. She says yes, tentatively. I explain
that the uncle is nowhere around, and that Jan is fully grown up
now; Jan is no longer in the same vulnerable situation and really
needs her help. As she smiles shyly, an angel sweeps in to remove
the last vestige of darkness in her chest. Her face flushes with
happiness.*

*The little girl shows me a transparent image of herself
growing up to Jan's age; then she returns to the form of a five-
year-old. This tells me that she is healed fully, but still needs to
meet my client at that younger age. Both of them will grow
mutually through Jan's experiences and healing. She commits to
helping Jan fully transform with her.*

*My power animals put her in a safe place and direct my
attention to the beginning of the soul loss. I notice a little girl
with no face. She is dancing, and then becomes surrounded in
darkness and is afraid to move. All of this tells me that her
family did not know her for who she is and that their emotional
aura did not allow her to express herself. I am told that she*

started to contemplate leaving at age two and a half and finally left around three and a half years of age.

We send her up to the healing angels. When she returns, her hair is a pale, shiny blonde, and she moves her body constantly. Jan's hair is dark brown, so the blonde color is probably a metaphor for an optimistic attitude and a spiritual quality that is vibrant with Spirit. My power animals and I ask her why she left and what quality she carries. She said she left because her parents made her feel it was bad to be and express who she is. She says that she carries the quality of Spirit-connection. I ask her if she is ready to return and if she will see the integration through to transformation. She says yes. I question why she is not fully grown. My power animals say that she carries much energy, which Jan will need to get used to; she needs to introduce that energy to Jan little by little. She will grow up quickly, within Jan.

I ask the soul parts what signal they will give Jan to get her attention even during the busiest of times. They say it is the sensation of her hair standing up on end at her crown chakra.

The signal gets past the "same old, same old" emotions that she might otherwise mistake for her own, not realizing that the soul parts are trying to get her attention. Without the signal, they would go inside her emotions, stir them up, and direct her to notice someone nearby – as if to say, "See? This guy is behaving just like my uncle did and that is why I left!" Or, "That woman is just as restricting as my mother was!" Then she would have issues with those people, even though those people did nothing. This is called "projection." Soul parts use it BIG time, if we do not pay attention to them. The signal averts this and helps our healing progress more easily and gently.

My power animals put Jan's three soul parts into a special spiritual container, to keep their energy separate from mine. We travel back to my spirit teacher. I ask my teacher if there are anyone else's soul parts attached to Jan. He says yes: parts of her uncle and parents are on her head, chest, and along her left arm. He tells me to work with her to change destructive beliefs about herself and life; these will become evident as we work with the soul parts during the transformation process.

My teacher says there are still five or six core soul parts still missing. I ask, "Why are you vague about the number?" He says. "It all depends upon the purpose of the next soul retrieval. Some of those core parts could meld together into one image, depending upon what spiritual quality she wishes to retrieve."

He advises that she is to keep a diary of her attitudes, actions, views, and emotional thoughts over the next several weeks, drawing a star (*) next to any that are different or unusual. She is also to jot down anything that is new. She is not to discount any of her experiences, no matter how subtle or dramatic. This awareness will tell her whether the soul parts are active or passive in her life.

Now I ready myself to return to the middle world. I thank my spirit teacher, power animals, and Jan's High Self for their help. I take the container of soul parts and carefully carry them back down from the upper world.

I move off the couch where we were sitting side by side. I ask Jan to lie down on her back and to envision herself as a hollow vessel, welcoming her soul parts into her being. I blow them into her, literally and symbolically. I notice a burst of energy and a strong sense of direction from them, each choosing a different place of residence within her body. I shake a special rattle around her body until the soul parts are permanently anchored in; this assures that they will not leave before we can work with their full integration.

It is then that I tell her what transpired during my journey. She weeps when I describe the incident with her uncle; she knows he had abused her emotionally. She has no memories of the incident I describe, but it strikes a resonance of truth within her.

During the first integration session a few days later, the age five soul parts fill in the details: For the umpteenth time, the uncle had taunted her about the worthlessness of girls. Even so, she sensed his tormented soul and desperately cried out, "God loves you! God loves you!" He pushed her down to the ground and the shock of the action jolted the "feeling-connection to God" soul part out of her body. (The "Spirit connection" soul part loosened the link for "feeling-connection," when that one left at the age of three.) Her uncle jeered scornfully, "Can God help you now?! He isn't strong enough to stop me from doing this, is he?! God is dead!" The energy of his actions, his jeering words, the humiliation of his emotional vibration, and "feeling-connection" leaving, traumatized her. Her heart sank and the soul part carrying Hope also left. From that point onward she felt like the dirt she fell onto that day, and felt the dirtiness of her uncle's vibration. She truly believed she was like dirt: no good, unworthy, and powerless to believe anything else. This was the origin of her low self-esteem.

Results Of Retrievals

Described below are results of various clients' experiences with the results of soul retrievals. These accounts show how the spiritual quality that the soul part brings back adds a greater sense of competency and interest in a specific area of life. This ability feels very natural.

CASE STUDY of Mona (a composite character)
Mona came into my office with a pleasant but serious expression on her face. She was "all business" and dressed impeccably. She talked so quietly that I had a hard time hearing her. Her concern was a lack of joy and interest in life.

When I retrieved her soul parts, I found that her *true* issue was that she did not know how to play. She broke into tears when I told her this. She said that she could not bring herself to play with her toddler daughter. In fact, she could not even remember being able to play when she was a child.

When she returned for her first transformation session after the soul retrieval, she told me – with complete bewilderment – that Saturday morning she felt compelled to watch cartoons on TV. *All morning!* I responded, "Didn't I retrieve a three-year-old and a five-year-old for you? You were responding to *their* interests!" We broke out laughing.

CASE STUDY of Diane. Diane reported that the day after her soul retrieval, her age-twenty soul part made her clean house. This was a new impulse. She usually does not like to house-clean, but the impulse felt so natural that she went along with it.

CASE STUDY of Paula. Paula walked stiffly down the hall into my office. Her eyes were sunken and dark. She showed hardly any emotion and spoke very softly, telling me of her life-long bout with depression.

During the soul retrieval, I saw that the true cause of her depression was grief...grief for her beloved grandma who died when Paula was five years old, and grief for the soul parts that had left her to go be with her grandma. The returning soul parts brought a profound amount of energy back into Paula's physical being as well as spontaneously healing the grief, just by their sheer presence. She no longer had to grieve for them; they were home!

When she returned for her first transformation session several days later, her step was lighter, her eyes sparkled and she spoke enthusiastically. Her life-long depression lifted. She was totally amazed!

Her shamanic journey at the beginning of that first session reflected this change. In the journey, Paula and all four soul parts are in a circle, laughing and holding hands. Soul part age five asks Paula, "Want to dance?" Paula nods yes and they both dance. Age-Five continues, "I love you, I bring you messages of love." She also gives a warning: "Prepare, be ready. Journey. It is important to take care of yourself." Age-Five then grows up to Paula's age of forty-five.

Paula's Letter

Paula described her results in a letter two years after her first soul retrieval: "I am thankful for the healing I have received from our first session together, which was truly life-saving and miraculous. I came to you in the midst of a horrible bout with depression, a life threatening and debilitating disorder that I had put up with all of my life. The treatment was indeed immediate and permanent, and even the extreme ups and downs of life in the last two years have not changed my essential and complete healing.

"I cannot describe to many people what this feels like, to be free of the knapsack of rocks that depression forced me to carry. I see the world with more clarity even as I experience my own emotions with a little more detachment. I could go on and on. There were two tough periods for me in the last two years. First the initial grieving I had to do over the loss of those four decades of my life. I was celebrating my strength for surviving, but mourning the wasted years, especially my girlhood and young adult years that were given over to so many months of suicidal fog. It was a grieving as intense as any I have ever gone through and I feel mostly on the other side of it. The second tough time was the first major crisis I had after the soul retrieval. It threatened to plunge me back into the old familiar behavior patterns! But I realized that the *experience* of depression is different from the behaviors of it, and I can now pull myself out of the behaviors since I am no longer experiencing the feelings.

"Thank you for guiding and facilitating me through this. You have given me a new life!"

Frequently Asked Questions

• *Can all the soul parts come back at the same time?*

No. Imagine that eighty soul parts have left, from age three to a year ago. Now imagine all of them back right now, still appearing as the age at which they left. Now imagine all of them demanding our attention and action...*right now!* And then getting upset with you for not doing their bidding...*right now!* Overwhelming, yes?

Retrieving a few soul parts at a time is safer and easier to handle. When they have transformed within you, they perhaps can draw back other parts when the time is right.

• *Does a soul retrieval happen every time we go for one?*

When I am given the "go ahead" from my spirit teacher, it always does. If my teacher says I am not to do one, then I do not retrieve soul parts. Once in a while he says that the person needs another form of therapy, spiritual healing, or further journeying before they are ready. In two instances the person's High Self said that a soul retrieval would actually be detrimental, due to karmic lessons the persons needed to experience from their major mental illness. Instead of a retrieval, their High Self and my spirit teacher gave detailed insights regarding how they could work with their problems, in order to meet the objectives Spirit intended for this life.

• *Will the parts leave again?*

Usually no, rarely yes. The soul parts will bear with us during the soul-transformation process. Chances are they persevered for months or years before they initially left. They will continue to help us in that same way, now that life circumstances are improved. However, if we return to the same type of situation that caused them to leave in the first place, and we do not try to get out of it, they may choose to leave again.

A hypothetical example: "Beulah's" soul part left due to physical abuse from her father. Now she is in a physically abusive relationship with a boyfriend, so the soul part strongly urges her to leave him. If she ignores the soul part and chooses to stay there, it will leave again. The soul part did not put up with abuse before; she certainly will not do so now.

You also can choose to send them away again, if you do not value yourself enough to go inward to nurture your soul parts and take their advice, and if you do not want them nagging at you. But I strongly advise against sending them away. It may seem simple to allow the soul parts to leave again. It is not. It is actually *very painful.* The emotional discomfort, foreboding and fear leading up to soul loss leave their residue behind when the soul part leaves; added to this is the loss of valuable soul qualities and vital essence. Painful feelings are your soul part's cry for help. If you do not value yourself enough to do the work on your own, that in itself is *your* cry for help. Both are indications that the healing work is incomplete. That is why I strongly advocate transformation work to begin within the week following the soul retrieval, and to occur frequently within the first month...whether the work be on your own or facilitated by your shamanic practitioner.

CHAPTER 5

INITIAL STAGES OF TRANSFORMATION

Integration Or Transformation?

At first I called soul retrieval follow-up "integration." But that term does not quite convey the depth of what I have found is preferable in bringing a soul part back into one's being.

According to Webster's New Collegiate Dictionary, 1956 edition, the psychological meaning of integration can be: "a. Co-ordination and relation of the total processes of perception, interpretation, and reaction insuring a normal, effective life. b. Harmonious co-ordination of behavior and personality with one's environment." In the same dictionary, "integrate" means "to form into a whole, to unite, unify or give the sum total of."

In reference to soul retrievals, these descriptions do not necessarily mean that much change occurs in the person after a soul retrieval. They merely infer that what was once incomplete has now been brought into a greater whole within the environment of that person. In other words, their soul parts are back, along with their spiritual qualities and are connected to the whole, to some degree. It does not necessarily mean that the person's issues are healed and transformed.

This same dictionary defines "transform" as: "To change in structure or composition; rarely, to transmute. To change in nature, disposition, heart; to convert."

The methods and insights given to me by Spirit actually begin to transform you after each soul retrieval, completing said transformation when all or nearly all of the missing soul parts are returned and worked with effectively. This means you are better off, spiritually, than before the soul parts originally left.

What Does All This Mean?

As defined above, "integration" does not quite convey the depth of what actually happens after a soul part is returned. Yes, some degree of integration occurs regardless of whether we work at it or not; soul parts *always* fully integrate into the emotions and feelings. However, there is more to us than that. We have beliefs, attitudes, habits and ways of acting in which the soul part may or may not be in sync. How that soul part initially fits in with the whole may determine your attitude regarding whether or not you feel like you even need a follow-up. Your feelings may or may not reflect reality. Here are a variety of common experiences from soul retrieval recipients:

(1) *Feeling totally integrated with the soul part*, you may think you do not need to return for a follow-up, and that doing so would be a waste of your time and money.

• *Complete access.* Some people have said that their experience was absolutely wonderful and they did not have to return to the practitioner for integration work. They had instant and continued use of the spiritual quality, they felt more whole, and continued to feel vibrant from it many months later. This last phrase is the clue that the soul part may indeed be fully in. Note, however, my personal experience of those thirty+ parts that initially needed no integration, yet years later I was told by Spirit that I was then to integrate them more deeply.

• *Open communication.* Many people, when returning for their first soul-transformation session, say their soul parts are openly active in their lives. They report feeling better, more vibrant, even happier. They describe the numerous ways that the soul parts have communicated with them and helped them in their lives. When we worked together, this inner communion deepened, revealing beneficial aspects that they did not realize were there.

• *Initial energy subsides.* Some people said their soul parts were very active in their lives; they felt better, more vibrant, even happier. Consequently they delayed their first follow-up. When finally arriving to their first session they said that the initial burst of energy and communication had subsided. As we worked on the transformation process, the soul parts helped them know how to keep the strengths vitalized.

• *Surprisingly innate feelings.* My client Bob described how he went out to a restaurant alone, the evening after his soul retrieval. He was astounded how natural and easy it felt, in comparison to his former pattern. Previously, he would have stayed home if he could not find anyone to accompany him to a restaurant.

He also thought his integration was complete, because of this and a few other traits that were instantly accessible to him. However, a few weeks later he reported a lot of painful emotions coming up. These, we found, were connected to memories the soul parts were trying to give him that he considered very disturbing. Bob's experience shows how the transformation process can work in layers. Sometimes it seems to be complete; then it spirals into a cycle of bringing up new information and memories.

(2) You doubt your improvements. Some people recognize the positive changes in their lives since the soul retrieval. Yet they also try to explain it away to other forms of inner work they have been doing. They say, "After all, I have been working on this for a long time and it has probably only now sunk in." I say to them, "Yes, you have been working on the issue, but that work didn't click in until the soul retrieval. The soul part had to return in order to make your previous work effective and permanent in your life."

Perhaps another reason why anyone would doubt the presence of the soul part is because of a deep familiarity that accompanies the new quality. They think the familiarity is the signal of "same old" in their experience.

Every soul part carries part of a spiritual quality that it knows how to use in an innate way. The soul part carries the feeling of that innateness into our feeling nature. Thus, sensitive, self-knowing, aware people realize there is a difference while many other people do not. When I ask the latter about the soul part's qualities and the issues the retrieval addressed, they often suddenly recognize the soul part is indeed present and active. Because of its incredible innateness, they felt like it had always been there or was the result of other work they had done. That "always-been-there" sense was true for the soul part, but not really for my client. Because of the innateness, it is easy to be deceived into assuming that nothing came of the soul retrieval. If you cease inner work with the soul parts at this point you will run the risk of problems later. This is because you will tend to ignore the soul part when it tries to present new material and new concerns.

(3) No communication. If this is true for you, you may think the soul retrieval did not take effect. You may think, "Why should I throw good money after bad?" Here are several examples of a lot of people who experienced no initial communication.

• *Unrecognized communication.* For some people, the soul parts do not seem to communicate. When I ask them questions concerning the spiritual qualities that I was told about during the soul retrieval, they usually respond that many of those qualities are indeed more active in their lives. Surprised at realizing that, they also recognize how subtle and *innate* the traits are. The innateness is a feeling exuded by the soul part; the traits are innate to it even if not to you.

• *No communication.* There are instances in which the soul parts indeed do not communicate with my client after the soul retrieval, and do not share their spiritual qualities. After the first follow-up, the person realized why the soul parts had not been active. It was because my *client* needed further healing. The soul parts were either in hiding until that healing occurred, or they flat out refused to come in contact with the person until the healing was done. They did not put up with an intolerable situation in childhood and they were not about to put up with it within my client now that they were back!

• *Too controlling?* Some people do not think their soul parts are communicating when they actually are. During our first follow-up session the soul parts express frustration at trying to get my clients' attention, to no avail. When these clients acquiesce to experience the spiritual qualities the way *the soul parts* perceive them, not how my clients see them, these people are astounded at the difference between their previous view of the quality and what the soul parts now show them. Now that they understand *at a feeling level* what the quality is like, they are able to allow the soul parts' influence in their lives.

(4) *Strong or overwhelming emotions* usually propel people to return for the first follow-up on schedule. They want healing.

• *Projection (seeing your own worst fault in someone else).* Their strong emotions relate to the issues that the soul part knows the person needs to confront and heal. People who choose not to return for the follow-up are usually deeply invested in maintaining those issues; they refuse to give them up. Most people, however, do choose to return for follow-up. They find quick relief from the strong emotions after we work together, using methods written in this book.

• *Fear of the spiritual quality* can occur when a person's family rejected or punished them, as a child, for using it. That fear continues to last into adulthood. It is possible to request the return of the quality yet not realize the full perimeters that would be involved. In order to heal them and their experiences, we work with changing dysfunctional beliefs and attitudes. In some cases they also must commit to taking action in ordinary reality. Calling on the help of the soul parts and the spirit helpers is of significant support here.

(5) Working only on issues, to transform. *The soul part is YOU, not a thing.*

• Some people initially view their soul part as a "thing" or as energy separate from who they perceive themselves to be. They choose to work only on issues, abstractly, rather than interact with the soul part as a peer. One man was surprised to discover that his soul part is as multidimensional as he is. Several women's spirit helpers told them "Be not afraid of your soul part. After all, she is you!"

Occasionally, working on issues *is* what is needed. This is the exception, not the rule, though. Keep in mind that it is our *soul parts*, not just the issues, that need the help

(6) No follow-ups. Many people have reported a lot of pain or numbness when they do not have follow-up work with their soul part.

• *Problems and Pain.* At several of my lectures on soul retrieval, a few people have asked me to talk about what happens when a person neglects their soul part. After I described my observations, these same people told the group that they had had a lot of problems with their soul part because their practitioner did not help them know how to work with it. One person related his deeply painful experience since his soul part left in soul loss once again. This happened because he did not know how to work with it.

• *Turbulent Emotions.* Several people have scheduled sessions with me in order to heal turbulent emotions coming from a soul retrieval given by someone else. Their practitioner had not helped them communicate with the soul part. In each instance, they received healing from the work we did together, using the methods revealed in this book.

• *Repeat-Soul-Loss.* Several people came for soul retrievals and divulged that they had had a soul retrieval from someone else. They were quite certain that those soul parts had left once again. In one case, my spirit teacher told me to find and retrieve the soul part that had left, in addition to retrieving ones that addressed the issue the person wanted healed.

(7) Delayed reactions.

• *Soul parts may delay sharing.* Some clients seemed to have completed the transformation process. Then, a few weeks or months later they returned for another soul retrieval. My spirit helpers informed me that the person needed to work further with the previous soul parts; it was too soon to get another retrieval.

The soul parts had additional information or new healing needs that were important to tend to.

• *"Jigsaw puzzle" soul pieces.* There are times when another soul retrieval is needed in order to fully integrate the previous soul parts. An analogy: this is much like doing a jigsaw puzzle. We may have a key piece (soul part) in hand, but that key piece needs the other pieces around it in order to lock into the picture itself.

Emotional Integration Is Automatic!

In all of the above illustrations, the emotional or feeling factor plays a primary role in whether or not my client thinks that the soul parts are there. It is crucial to realize that ***emotional integration is automatic for all soul parts at the time of the soul retrieval.*** However, emotional integration does not mean the healing is complete. Emotions are strictly indicators of what is happening within us, according to the values that we as Spirits have constructed for our life. Full emotional integration is why: you may have instant access to the soul part's strengths and feel dramatically better...or why you may not feel anything, because you are used to suppressing your feelings...or why you get more upset than usual over your issues.

Your emotions after the soul retrieval tell you the state of your soul part and how well it feels it fits within you. After a while, the soul part may choose to convey a concern it previously kept hidden but now wants you to attend to. If you choose to ignore the soul part, it may refuse to give you access to its strengths, or refuse to communicate at all until you make necessary changes, or put up such a fuss that you feel like your life is worse now than before the retrieval. If you do nothing to alleviate its concerns, it will leave again on its own or you may choose to send it away.

When you tend to the soul part's needs, you will find that your emotions become more peaceful or joyous. That says that transformation has begun.

These circumstances indicate that the soul part has indeed integrated to some degree, accessing some aspects of your individuality. But that does not necessarily mean that you have complete and sustained use of the qualities the soul part returns to you, nor that the process is complete.

Analogies

At the emotional stage, integration is like living in a community with different races living next door to each other, each having different life styles. They may or may not try to get along, and they can leave at any time they choose.

Communication and cooperation between you and your soul part are the beginning stages of integration and transformation. *An analogy:* An orchestra has different instrumental qualities that work to attain finely tuned harmony and expression. The players may be committed for a while but they can still leave, thus hindering the orchestra's performance.

Full integration and transformation can occur in the same way, but have distinctly different effects. *An analogy:* mixing dye into water. You and the soul part take on the qualities of each other, intermixing and blending; you balance and strengthen each other.

With integration, this *analogy* is like the dye or the water being muddy. There is little or no change for the better. Emotional outbursts tell you this is so. The soul part can still leave if it or you choose such.

With transformation, this *analogy* is like the dye and the water being pure. The soul part and you are blended in full accord; it cannot leave again, regardless of the situation faced. The soul part also keeps you away from potential dangers in your environment and relationships. You instinctively know what and who to avoid as well as those you are safe to be drawn towards.

An analogy: Soul retrieval is like bringing a new child into a household. The child, most of the time, will stay. But do you expect that just because you birthed it you do not have to take care of it? Can the baby tend to its own needs and grow up completely on its own without your having to nurture and care for it? Do you want a harmonious family, or do you want one where there is alienation and strife? So it is with integration.

In bringing back a soul part, we gain use of some of its energy and feel more complete. But if we are not healed and transformed by the process, its energy will not allow the spiritual qualities to act instantly, innately and on command. It may even magnify our faults and shadow issues; in that case, the soul retrieval leads to the acquiring of disjointed and warring soul parts.

Spirit wants us to strive for total harmony. With this view, soul retrieval is not an end in itself, but merely a means to that end. The end we seek with the soul retrieval is actually the healing of the issue itself. *An analogy:* Healing is not like putting iodine on a cut and having to put up with the sting for a while. Instead, it is "making well," i.e., returning to a pristine condition.

Why Is Follow-up Important?

In tribal cultures, people were well acquainted with the concept of soul loss and soul retrieval. Therefore, anytime anyone showed signs of soul loss, the shaman would do a soul retrieval. This usually occurred within days of the loss; little attention to integration was needed, because the person did not have time to adopt dysfunctional ways. Because of the miniscule delay between loss and retrieval, full integration with all levels of the person's being took place swiftly and automatically. The person felt vibrant, complete, and able to access talents and strengths. If there were traumatic emotions connected to the soul loss cause, the tribe and shaman were there to help, immediately.

Conversely, in our twenty-first century society the concept of soul retrieval is radically new, resurrected only since the late 1980's. Since soul retrieval was not known in mainstream healing arts and medical practices prior to that time, everyone who has suffered soul loss has had to adapt to feeling less adept, less whole, and less alive. We have had to put up with the lack of certain commonly held human traits, often not realizing that the spiritual characteristics are our birth-right, much less knowing we could reclaim them. We humans are very adaptable, but with soul loss we adapt into dysfunctional beliefs, attitudes and ways of being. Adapting to "less than" leads to dysfunctional ways to which we have become accustomed. The longer we reside in dysfunctional habits, the harder it is to break their ingrained hold. Dysfunction becomes imbedded in the subconscious mind at subliminal levels where we have no conscious control over it. In other words, others can "push our buttons" and we become momentary automatons, acting out the subliminal programming. Because of these deeply imbedded ways, much more attention to transformation, *at a deep, energetic, attitudinal, belief level,* is required in order to bring us into a more pristine condition. In essence, the transformation process advances us forward on the evolutionary path, more than we were at the time of the soul loss.

Receiving a soul retrieval, alone, may or may not be enough to affect full healing. It may or may not bring us into the pristine use of our spiritual qualities and energy at a higher level than before. In my experience, the following variations may occur:

• there are some cases in which the soul retrieval alone *may* break the habit, purely because the habit's purpose is to hold the space until the "real thing" returns home. When this happens, you feel a change at once;

• if you have done extensive work on the issue, the soul retrieval may or may not be the only element remaining to heal you. If it is, you feel immediate change. If it is not, you will need to do further transformational work. Only after the retrieval can you know which of these paths is true for you;

• you may have to strive to use the spiritual qualities that the soul part brings home. The soul part may be comfortable with them, but *you* may not be. Letting go of any resistance to them is important;

• you personally may need to heal from the soul loss incident and its resultant effects. The soul part can help, if it was fully healed prior to the soul retrieval. But you still have to cooperate with it;

• you and the soul part may need healing of dysfunctional habits, attitudes and beliefs;

• complete healing is vital for full innate access to the returned spiritual qualities. This is part of transformation.

Another reason for the necessity of transformation work is that the moment the soul part leaves, its growth is arrested. It remains at the age, emotional state and mindset it was in at the moment of leaving. It is not able to communicate with you nor with other soul parts that leave. It cannot benefit from your experiences and growth. This means that when it is brought back home it joins a soul and body that is many years older than it was used to. The body feels different. Thought, attitudes, emotions and life circumstances are different. It has to form communication links with the rest of your soul. It may not be able to access all of your memories without your conscious consent. Likewise, you cannot access the soul part's strengths, qualities and memories unless the soul part allows such. The following two case studies illustrate how this works.

CASE STUDY *of Karen.* My client Karen's third soul part (named "Three"), when she grew up to age thirty within Karen, was amazed at the changes made by the other two soul parts that had returned at the same time she did. "Three" had not been aware of the changes the other two were making during their healing process! Maybe she was lost in thought, absorbed in her own private world?? This clearly indicates that soul parts do not necessarily access memories automatically, much less be cognizant of our doings!

CASE STUDY of *Sophie.* My client Sophie's "Caring" soul part tried to take over various jobs, beyond the capacity of her soul quality. "Caring" thought she was supposed to "stand up for" Sophie, in a gentle meek way, as she used to do prior to soul loss. (In childhood, "Caring" took over the job of assertive parts that had already left.) Clearly, she was not in communication with Sophie's other soul parts. If she were, she would have known that the assertive ones were back, assuming their rightful roles.

When there is no follow-up, or you shy away from same, the soul part becomes essentially an "orphan." Initially you may gain use of its energy, feel more complete and perhaps have access to the soul part's spiritual qualities. Thus you consider it to be completely integrated and not needing any special attention. You ignore its pleas for attention and perhaps assume that all you need do is work on issues. However, improvement may be short-lived and you lose ready access to the soul part's spiritual qualities. If you heal, it may take years. You may repress feelings or live in fear. Emotional turmoil, projection, trying to "fix" others and current situations create relationship havoc.

> *Without healing and transformation work,*
> *problems may occur because:*
> *Either you or the soul part assumes leadership*
> *without the other's consent,*
> *Or there is constant conflict between you and the soul part.*

Inner work endeavors to create sacred space and community *within you.* If there is not full harmony and cooperation among parts of one human, that person cannot attain full harmony and cooperation with other humans. Full healing occurs at an *energetic level,* rather than through intellectual meandering or surface level ritual. Once the inner healing occurs, it is easier to enact outer ritual and to behave in new ways outwardly. In other words, mindfulness of the soul part is more easily attained after you have worked with the soul part at deep levels, like on a shamanic journey or in alert trance.

Just Work On Your Issues!

It may seem that after a soul retrieval all you need do is to work on issues that arise, and by doing so you will bring the soul part fully into your being. But that is a misunderstanding of the process. It is our *soul parts*, not just the issues, who need your help.

To illustrate, let us say that you came back to live with your family after a ten-year absence in which you had had absolutely no communication with them. Would you not want everyone to welcome you, to ask about your experiences and you about theirs? Would you not expect everyone to take time to get to know each other again? How would you feel if they talked only about their agendas, expected you to flow with their expectations without question, and to not take the time to ask you what special gifts you have to contribute to the family effort? If you took the initiative to speak up in favor of your objectives, how would you feel if they ignored you or repressed your expression? Would you not feel like they viewed you as an object rather than a person? Would you not feel like you wanted to leave again?

That is the situation with your returned soul part. It is every bit the unique individual that you are. It wants to be appreciated and valued, just as you do. After all, it *is* you!

After the soul retrieval, working on issues alone is too general a method. It is much like cleaning the whole house in hopes of finding one specific item. That is a process of trying to heal from the outside in. It takes a long time and may or may not result in change. Conversely, soul transformation focuses specifically on the soul part, healing from the inside out. The soul part knows what specific events and issues the person needs to heal. That is like going to the specific spot in the house where the lost item is. When the specific event and reaction are healed, there may no longer be any need for the generalized issue, so it magically dissipates.

It is imperative to work directly with the soul part and its unique intelligence, during the integration and transformation process. To not do this is to ignore or crassly manipulate your self. In working directly with the soul part, you approach each spiritual quality and each feeling as a person (soul part), not a thing (spiritual quality). The methods Spirit gave me achieve this by bringing about a cooperative balance among all personal traits without denying or repressing any aspect of self.

There are deceptive elements of a soul retrieval that can make you think that issues work alone can help, when it really is better to work directly with the soul part. They are:

· Familiar feelings and "same old" emotions that make you think everything is as it was before the retrieval and the soul retrieval did not take hold. In the beginning, most of the feelings that arise are actually communications from the soul part.

· "Same old" situations and issues can also make you think that life is "business as usual" and that the soul part is dormant or not actually there. Issues that throw you into projection are especially suspect. Projection is a very common tool the soul part uses to get your attention when you do not listen to the soul part's communication.

· The soul part's quality may be subtle and difficult to focus on. Subtleties are easy to dismiss especially if you have "control issues" or are used to repressing feelings. The soul part is one small part of you; if it feels that small, its feelings and spiritual quality also feel that small within you. When you open up to the soul part and it to you, the subtleties grow, becoming large and dynamic.

· The soul part exudes a sense of naturalness to using an ability. If you examine it closely and compare it to your experience prior to the retrieval, you realize that it is a *new* ability that you are experiencing or that the old ability has a new dimension to it. You have to compare before-and-after, to discern this.

· Psychotherapists say that slow work is safer. That is wise when you have not had a soul retrieval. Resilience and strength are important traits to cultivate, to withstand traumas that would otherwise throw you into emotional turmoil.

However, the exact opposite tack is true when you have had a soul retrieval. The returned soul part is like an infant; you would not let a baby cry for hours or days on end without tending to it. Going slowly is like letting the baby cry; *going slowly re-traumatizes* you and the soul part! It is not going to put up with unacceptable conditions for long. It *will escalate* issues and turbulent emotions in your life, until you attend to its needs. It left once before; it will leave again if you ignore it and its needs.

With soul integration, faster more immediate work is safer.

Preparation For Soul Retrieval?

How fast the transformation process progresses depends upon your readiness as well as the readiness of your soul part. This may mean that you will need to work on the soul loss issue ahead of obtaining a soul retrieval. But sometimes there is no possible way to prepare adequately because the soul part takes most or all memory of the soul loss incident with it when it departs. Even if you do hypnotherapy sessions to "the cause of low self-esteem," for example, you may not find any anchoring point for healing. The appropriate memories are gone.

> *CASE STUDY of Rosalee.* Reflect on the story of my client Rosalee's experience as described in the "Soul Loss" chapter. Her soul part left due to an argument she had with a close friend in the eighth grade. Only when Rosalee did a shamanic journey to the soul part, did it bring to her awareness the memory of an *inner* incident which she did not recall ever having in physical life nor prior to the soul retrieval. She saw *three* images of her friend Milly all at the same time; it was clear that these were Milly's soul parts hanging onto Rosalee.
>
> The point here is that the soul parts flung at Rosalee by her friend were a major cause of her low self-esteem. They escaped detection until the soul retrieval. I had already worked with Rosalee to release other people's soul parts from her aura without finding the three cited above. Her subconscious mind could not discover threads of memory leading to them until the soul retrieval occurred. Only a soul retrieval could restore her memory enough to be able to work on the true cause of her low self-esteem.

With other people and in other circumstances, memory has a different effect. Some people are astonished at how minor the soul loss incident seems. A common response is, "I cannot believe that *this* simple incident could have caused soul loss!" The crucial memories were not in the subconscious, so they could recall only the more benign aspects of the occurrence. When they commenced with the transformational process, the soul part revealed more memories and understanding about the incident, such that revealed the significance of the event.

An incident causing soul loss may be as innocuous as a slight frown on Mama's face, going into the church nursery for just one hour, or leaving Grandma after a wonderful visit. The soul part may bring back memories that directly relate to a chosen career or spiritual life path. As a result, the person realizes they had felt like they were leaving a wonderful experience that was crucial to their heart and, ultimately, to their life's mission. They felt that the new situation was in some way sabotaging their deepest longing. To their *spirit,* the change was untenable. Therefore, soul loss was the only option.

In such cases, there is no guarantee that previous psychological work would bring up such seemingly trivial incidents as being the cause of fear or lack of joy. We may be so used to thinking that only dramatic occurrences can have a profound effect on us, so we ignore or discount the subtle cues. Spiritual issues may seem subtle on the surface, yet when they are fully resolved and healed, there is profound impact.

If you have done extensive spiritual growth work, making considerable improvement in specific issues, the only component left may be to get a soul retrieval. You may not need any follow-up. You would have experienced improvement prior to the retrieval and innate access to the spiritual qualities and vibrant essence afterwards. There would be no residue of the issue, and Spirit may actually say, "this is the end of the matter."

At other times, it may be important to pay attention to the transformational process with your new soul parts. You may feel that the soul parts are integrated in you yet you realize you are still working on your issues. *These are NOT two different things.* They fit together like hand-in-glove. If you work only on the issues, you will find it is a never-ending process much like trying to bail water out of a boat that has a leak in the bottom of it. Conversely, if you focus on only the soul part and heal it, your issues disappear rapidly just as bailing water out of a boat occurs rapidly once the hole is sealed.

Soul parts are not fully integrated/transformed as long as your issues are not healing.

For most people receiving a soul retrieval, the breakthrough is at the beginning of the healing, rather than at the end of it, as occurs with a lot of talk therapy. That is because our transformation process focuses specifically on the soul part and its reason for leaving. Since we now know the exact incident and issue to work with, we no longer have to guess at what started the problem. We know! In addition, we have the intelligence and memories of the newly returned soul part to help us bring about full healing. Healing and inner growth progress rapidly and smoothly.

Rapid healing, however, does not mean glossing over necessary aspects. That would be a form of denial, which leads to a lot of emotional and attitudinal problems down the road. If we try to integrate the soul part without getting in touch with its spiritual qualities and healing the issues regarding why it left, transformation is subverted.

> **CASE STUDY** of Lynne: For many months Lynne had suffered with an unhealed, un-integrated soul part that had returned spontaneously through another form of healing work. Yet it took less than two hours of facilitated work to transform her life experience. She wrote:
>
> "This is just so cool, everything is so clear." I remember saying this during the experience of my soul transformation session while connected to my High Self and my power animals. It was just unbelievable, and yet believable because it was happening!
>
> "A few weeks earlier, I had virtually inhaled Maryphyllis's information on soul transformation. Her words fed a place in me that cried out for attention. She wrote that you could do decades of healing in a single session and that tore right through to the depths of my soul. I have been on a deep healing path for almost a decade, and although I have had incredible breakthroughs with many great healers from around the world (many well-known and published), I have always felt like something was simply not being touched upon.
>
> "I consider myself young (in my early forties), yet I have been blessed with many physical and emotional challenges to try to make me pay attention to the emotional and spiritual sides of my physical health. I spent a great deal of my daily life in bed for several years, not living my life, basically just surviving. I made great progress with many healing modalities along with herbs, supplements, diet and yoga to bring my physical health to a much better place. Still, something continued to say look deeper.
>
> " I took Maryphyllis's shamanic journeying workshop and then obtained a private session. This transformation session dealt with a soul part that had come back to me

spontaneously several months ago; I was aware that that soul part was not integrated and was aggravating my emotional and physical problems.

"Here is the email I sent Mayphyllis the night after that session: *It is after midnight, way past my bedtime and I am still feeling energized. When I first met with you today, I was really tired and had planned on coming back home and taking a nap. Instead, I came back and put on some music, cranked up the stereo and danced and sang and felt like I was just electrified; it was quite amazing to have so much energy, spirit and fun!*

I appreciate your helping me to grow my soul part up to my age. I do have flashes of her as the little girl in the corner, but I feel like it is because that was such a sad vision. It may take me a while to get it out of my head. I also can see her at my age, still looking out of my eyes. So, I just wanted to thank you again.

"It has now been two weeks since my lower world journeying class with you and almost a week since my soul transformation session. Each day I find myself more and more in awe at how my life has been changed in such a short amount of time. I am waking up with conviction to begin my day instead of wondering how to get up and then how to get through it. Prior to this session, I was dealing with a lot of issues revolving around fear, emotional turbulence, mood swings, etc. It felt like I was walking in mud, stuck and unable to complete or even begin many simple projects. The soul transformation session returned many attributes that had been missing, such as peace of mind with renewed self-esteem, courage and backbone, the ability to speak my mind and best of all: self-love. I am now able to make decisions and feel good about them! My energy is wonderful and I have been tackling projects left and right. I feel as if I am looking at life from within myself instead of from above myself, like I had been previously. I feel stronger and have more energy for yoga and gardening and such. And I have had creativity flow through me with the grace of Spirit again. I am feeling quite alive. I am finding that while I am doing a better job of speaking up for myself, I am also lightening up and not taking myself so seriously. My days seem to be more fun.

"I am very grateful for Spirit's answer to my prayers to send me gentle medicine. I highly recommend soul transformation sessions. No matter where you are on your path, it is important to integrate all of the work that you have previously done. And it is so wonderful to have it be done gently and energizingly. It is amazing how Spirit is sending Maryphyllis the tools to quickly do decades of healing. She freed me from work I needed to do around age seven and age thirty, and it *all happened in a single session!* I would otherwise have spent another decade on each of those."

Complete VS Incomplete

Inner healing and deep communication with the soul parts is designed to make sure they help us live our life in such a way that they will not have cause to leave again. A very important aspect of soul transformation is to be able to communicate clearly with the new soul part and experience its spiritual qualities actively in our life. In everyday life some soul parts communicate with us very easily. That is because their nature is either an outgoing one or is familiar to us. This dramatic effect of soul retrieval is not necessarily a sign of full-integration, i.e., transformation. There may be subtle aspects present which are dwarfed by the dramatic elements; that may not show up until later.

> *CASE STUDY of Karen.* I retrieved three soul parts for my client Karen. When she returned a week later for her first follow-up session, she said these soul parts were already very active in her life. She resigned from one job that she disliked and had spontaneously obtained another job she was thrilled with. She also bought a house with many acres of country wilderness around it, a place she had yearned for, for many years but had not had the courage to buy. All of this in one week! And it felt so easy and natural to do!
> On the surface, it would seem that her soul parts were fully integrated, because they were so dynamically active in her life. However, on further discussion with her, she said she had some underlying fears that just would not go away. They had nothing to do with the changes she had made and she could not figure out what they were trying to tell her. When we began the exploratory process of transformation, we discovered that her fear came from knowing that at least one of the soul parts carried a highly sensitive and powerful psychic gift. She was terrified of it. We spent a lot of time healing the causes of this fear. The soul part's psychic quality

was subtle on the surface. It carried a profound undercurrent that has since been very dynamic in her life. Had we not attended to the subtlety, the soul parts could have eventually been destructive to Karen's peace of mind.

Because subtleties with soul parts are so easily ignored, yet have proved to be significant in many people's integration processes and lives, it is important to be able to recognize their presence. It is also important to recognize when a soul part is clamoring for attention, needing more healing, or wanting to tell us about some new facet of its spiritual quality.

In other words, how do we recognize if the integration and transformation is complete or not? The rest of this chapter contains information that can help you answer that question.

Projection

Projection is defined as: (1) Seeing our own worst faults or best traits mirrored in the other person. (2) We strongly object to or are attracted by traits and actions in another person but the true source of attraction originates within us.

Negative projection feels like we are over-reacting; we find our "buttons are being pushed" or that we are mentally arguing with that person. Anytime someone else's actions stir up our emotions, it is a signal that we are denying that a fault exists within us. For instance, our boss may seem to be as emotionally abusive as Dad was. For some people this may be the truth while for others it is an illusion. By illusion, I mean that the boss is not actually abusive; our projection only makes him seem that way.

In the soul transformation process, negative projection is a valuable tool. The soul part uses it to try to get our attention to the fact that it needs help. It gets inside our emotions, stirs them up, finds a situation that resembles the issue it is concerned with, and – in essence – cries out, "See! That is just like what happened to me before I left! *Do something!*" The moment that happens, it is important to go inward and attend to the needs of the soul part. The outer circumstance is usually coincidental. If you try to resolve *only* the current outer situation, nothing gets resolved. It is as futile as trying to bail out that proverbial rowboat that has a hole in the bottom of it.

The soul part uses projection when we are not responding to an agreed-upon signal...or we are ignoring it...or we refuse to go inward to pay attention to its needs.

PROJECTION: Take it Seriously.
Do not take it Personally!

When you feel your buttons are being pushed, take projection *seriously* by immediately assuming the soul part is trying to get your attention. At that moment, just reflect inward and ask what it wants to say or what it needs. If there is no response, the projection is probably just your issue, not the soul part's. If you are not sure, you can do a journey to the soul part and your spirit helpers.

When you feel your buttons are being pushed and you want only to resolve things with the other person, instead of going inward, you are taking projection *personally.* Do not take the button pushing personally. What is happening is not you. At the core, you are ok and one with Spirit. Emotions and reactions are an attention-getter and that is all. Use them as such, and strive to bring healing to yourself.

    Hypothetical Case Study of "Jake". Jake's soul part is grieving for a friend who died in childhood. However, Jake feels the love pain and thinks it relates to a current loved one rejecting him. No amount of therapy on the current situation will alleviate the grief. The only way to affect beneficial change is to listen to the soul part's concerns, express empathy and obtain healing for him and the past situation. Such brings "miraculous" healing to the current situation without even trying.

To heal projection from the soul part, allow the soul part to lead you to the soul loss event, wherever that may be and no matter how pressing the current pain is. Sometimes it is very compelling to want to stay with the current situation and try to heal its pain. That may be effective for current-day causes, but it does not work when you are dealing with a newly returned soul part. The soul part is very much in the present too, and exudes that sense of "now-ness". *However, its present moment is the present day of the age in which it left the body!* It may be age three while you are age forty. Healing *its* "present" will immediately uplift your mood. And, *your* "present" will miraculously heal all by itself!

What truly works is to focus on the soul part, despite the gargantuan pull to look at the current day problem. It is imperative to heal the soul part and its feelings, comfort and support it, get to know its strengths and how to implement them, and to also heal your own wounds around that long ago situation. Current circumstances then heal all by themselves.

Projection is a natural part of the healing and rapport process after the soul retrieval. Because the soul part has a penchant for developing problems, I like to obtain a signal that the soul part will give you to get your attention when you are distracted in life. This signal can be as simple as inwardly hearing a tone or word, or becoming aware of a color, or feeling an itchy earlobe. It usually is best that the soul part and you agree on the signal. Then, when it appears, immediately reflect inward with your thoughts and ask the soul part what it wants.

The signal often averts projection. Sometimes, though, both are used by the soul part. Either way, pay attention to the soul part!

Positive Or Negative Polarity?

The returning soul part usually has a self-honoring and decisive nature to it. In many cases that is why it left to begin with: it did not put up with a bad situation then and it is certainly not going to put up with it now that it is back! Whether that bad situation, now, shows up in outer relationships or in our thinking, the soul part is insistent on getting changes made. Using turbulent emotions and projection are the most common ways in which it tries to get our attention.

Faster healing and gentle integration occur when we listen to the concerns of the soul part, negotiate how and when to put changes into life activities, and allow spiritual healing to occur. When the soul loss circumstances are fully healed, we can more easily use our spiritual qualities in a way that feels natural. This ease and naturalness of action indicates that your soul part has a positive attitude regarding its interaction with you. It feels honored and useful.

If at any time you refuse to complete the inner work, or to repress the soul part, it will respond with negative attitudes and feelings, projection and the like. Turbulent emotions are not like a holistic healing crisis wherein you can just bide your time until it goes away, knowing that healing will result. *Turbulent emotions are actually a signal from the soul part that it needs help.* **It will continue to escalate its signals if you do not pay attention to it.**

Problems can manifest in any number of ways: relationship conflicts, projection, contradicting thoughts beyond what may have been the case prior to the soul retrieval, the lesser one (soul part *or* some aspect of you) becoming devious and sabotaging, inner power struggles, emotional turmoil, strengthening shadow aspects. If you ignore the soul part and its needs, it may decide to leave in soul loss, once again. If that happens, you may feel you are worse off than before the soul retrieval. *This is not pleasant!*

Further Signs Of Incomplete Transformation

There are numerous signposts throughout the integration and transformation process that indicate that the transformation is still incomplete. Everyone's situation is a little different, so the order shown below may not be the exact order you may experience in any one soul retrieval. The most common indicators are listed here:

• Turbulent emotions such as sorrow, depression or anger, that do not get resolved until you work directly with the returned soul part.

• Your life becomes a mirror of the circumstances surrounding the original soul loss, in other words, "Projection."

• You have a tendency to ignore your soul part's pleas for attention.

• You know how to journey or go into trance but find it difficult to get down to doing it. While not a signpost in and of itself, it *is* one if other aspects on this list are also part of your experience.

• The soul part refuses to communicate with you, especially during inner work. Communication can be by speech, telepathy, body language, giving you energy, or through pure knowing. If one mode does not work for you, check out all the others. You may just be missing the soul part's way of communicating. It is a problem only when none of the ways work.

• The soul part chooses to act as a guide rather than coming fully into your body. This is a signal that either you need to do more healing to prepare for its energy, or that it has a distorted belief or attitude about something to do with your life.

• The soul part is reluctant to express its spiritual qualities in your life, or you find yourself not having ready access to those qualities.

• Some of the spiritual qualities are active and expressive, but so are some of the negative thought patterns.

• You think you are bad, especially in conjunction with not being able to readily access the spiritual quality. The attitude says the soul part is in control of your feelings. "You are bad" may actually be the soul part recalling the soul loss incident or chastising you for not applying its spiritual quality. Talk to it to find out what is going on and what needs healing.

• The soul part does not want to grow up to the age you are now. Feeling that you do not want to be as old as you are may actually be a symptom of the *soul part* not wanting to grow up. Find out what there is about the older age that it objects to, and then heal that.

• In a journey or trance you see the soul part at a younger age. The soul part may have another concern it needs to heal, or it may be ready to share a new quality or aspect of a quality with you.

• You see your soul part as a separate individual, when you journey to it. This is especially significant if it still looks as young as it did when it first returned.

• You do not see your soul part as a separate individual, when you journey to it. However, you still hear or sense it individually.

Any of the above is a signal to continue to go inward to communicate with the soul part. If nothing happens, call a shamanic practitioner for a facilitated session. If you do nothing about it, the soul part *will* escalate your experience.

Levels Of Escalation
The soul part will try various ways to get your attention. The sooner you listen, the calmer and easier your integration process will be. The list here is arranged in order from calmest to most traumatic.

1. You pay attention to the soul part and honor its input in your life. ("Mindfulness")

2. The soul part gives you a prearranged signal to get your attention, when your mind is distracted. Then you pay attention to it.

3. The soul part projects its problems outwardly onto people who are close to you. ("Projection") This stage in itself can escalate with increasingly turbulent emotions.

4. The soul part represses its spiritual quality. It may feel like you do not want to use its spiritual quality, or your life feels unsafe to express the quality.

5. The soul part projects its problems outwardly onto everyone in your life. Your emotions are increasingly more turbulent.

6. The soul part evokes depression, anger, fear, and turbulence into your feeling-nature.

7. The soul part leaves again. This is an absolute last resort after many tries to communicate. Repeat soul loss is not a pleasant option to any hardship during the transformation process. Prior to its leaving, the soul part creates a lot of problems and turbulent emotions, all designed to be heard and to get its needs met. When it leaves, it not only takes away its energy, intelligent presence and spiritual qualities, it also leaves within you both fear and the everlasting residue of pain and turmoil it stirred up. In addition, it may take away memories; thus you cannot identify when, where and why the pain began. That prohibits any kind of lasting healing. In other words, it re-traumatizes you, leaving you worse off than before the soul retrieval!

CASE STUDY of *Paula.* My client Paula's experience illustrates what can happen, living with incomplete integration. Paula came in for a second soul retrieval a couple of weeks before she was to leave for a permanent job on another continent. She had already spontaneously retrieved a soul part. When I did a journey on her behalf, my spirit helpers said that the spontaneously retrieved soul part was enough to work with, without retrieving additional ones. The primary message from her soul part and her spirit helpers was that she needed to nurture her heart. They also said she needed to accept herself and that she was to not give away her power any longer.

We had time in her busy schedule for only two facilitated integration sessions. Her integration was only starting; it was by no means complete. A few days later she left for that job. Before she left I called her to ask how she was doing and asked her to please contact me any time she needed help.

Paula's Letter. In a letter a year and a half later, Paula describes her second soul retrieval. "I came to you for a second session and had quite a different experience from the first one. This time I was dealing with the other major issue in my life, which can only be summed up as Authority...in all its guises, but most especially in volatile relationships at work and in failure to have successful intimate relationships with adult men.

"During the sessions I had interesting, productive experiences. But events since then have proven that the healing is neither instant nor complete. I have had major work problems and a very special marriage has disintegrated! I am struggling with doing work that is well below my skill and educational level and I am devastated by the divorce.

" I congratulate myself that the despair did not throw me permanently into the Abyss of Depression, but it was close going.

"My soul parts (I converse regularly, but not daily), are bewildered by all this. My own heart and soul experienced such excruciating pain from the break up of my marriage that I gave control of them to my Guides and Power Animals. They are gathered in my power space in the Lower World. They are in a circle and usually face outwards. They look like they are guarding something in the middle of the circle. I (my soul) am lying in a fetal position on my side in the middle of the circle, covered by a thin blanket of leaves. My heart is buried in a locked gold case in the Earth right next to me. I would love your insight and wisdom."

My letter in response. In my letter responding to her, I described how to interpret the metaphorical images of journeying, how to do High Self healing, and four or five other methods. I also suggested she ask her primary spirit helper how to work with healing the soul part that is in the fetal position.

She responded, saying that my letter was very helpful. Right before she got it she realized she needed to check in with her "fetal" self more often. She tried one of the techniques I described and reintegrated this split-off part with the help of her other soul parts and spirit helpers.

In subsequent journeys she discovered several things. Her one-year-old soul part was the "pack leader" who now reassures the group. The group took a while to grow to her current physical age but she is in good spirits. Her journeys were concerned primarily with manifesting her gifts and talents.

Several years later she wrote saying that everything was going great and she was feeling well.

CHAPTER 6

SOUL TRANSFORMATION PRINCIPLES & METHODS

General Outline of Transformation Phases
- Emotional integration occurs at the soul retrieval.

From there, the following is in a generic order of process. Some phases may be switched according to a soul part's needs. In some cases, a phase may last as briefly as a few seconds while other phases may take days or weeks to progress through.

- Basic communication
  Rapport with the soul part
  Healing you and/or the soul part
  Rapport with the soul part's spiritual qualities
- Access Total Body And Mind
- Cleanse your aura
- Address your beliefs and attitudes
- Practical application with the soul part
- Permanent adulthood of the soul part
- Massive blending
  "Staying power" and "Leaving power"
  High Self blending
  Etheric web blending
- Core of your being
  Soul part enters when ready
  Purifying of the core

Principles Of Soul Transformation After Retrieval
- ***Emotions totally integrate at the soul retrieval.***
  *Negativity = the soul part needs attention **at once!***
  Innateness regarding a new trait comes from the soul part.
- ***Treat the soul part as a person, not a thing.***
  Soul part is a sentient feeling being just like you; it IS you!
  Enlist the soul part's help at every stage of transformation.
  Working just on issues = treating the soul part as a thing.
- ***Rapid progress is safer than slow progress.***

- *Take Projection seriously but not personally.*
- *Issues not healing? Integration isn't complete.*

Desired And Intended Outcome

Transformation of the soul part within you involves a multiplicity of facets. There is complete healing of your issue and its full access to all levels of your being: spirit, spiritual qualities, mind, memory, belief and attitude patterns, behavior, and emotions. There is infusion of the soul clear through your being and grown up to your age, i.e., not locked into earlier events. You have around-the-clock access to its qualities. You experience lasting healing from it, with no detrimental nor dysfunctional residue.

During the soul retrieval, Spirit has the option of healing the soul part so it will not bring back distorted attitudes, emotional pain and negativity that would make life worse than before. Even so, a major part of the follow-up process involves coordination between you and the soul part to help *you* heal. It is rare that a soul part will infuse completely into your being without this coordination. To repeat what I said earlier, soul retrieval is not an end in itself, but a means to an end: healing the issue you presented at the retrieval.

If full soul transformation does not occur within a month's time, your process is either incomplete or it is being subverted by something hidden. Sometimes, other soul parts may need to return in order to complete the healing and transformation of the present ones. Remember the jigsaw puzzle: you may have a key piece in your hand but cannot find its place because the ones it connects with are still missing from the picture. So it is with the process of transformation. Sometimes the key piece is a core soul part that makes sure all the other soul parts find their rightful link within us or can guide us more wisely. Usually, however, the process is simply not complete or there is a hidden subversion going on.

Transformation Phases

There is a wide diversity of experience regarding the soul retrieval integration/transformation process. Even multiple soul retrievals for the same person can be experientially diverse, sometimes totally opposite from previous ones. One soul part may need one aspect and order of work while another may require a quite different focus or organizational plan. Therefore it behooves us to look at and know the total process.

The order below is generally how most soul integration and transformation progresses. Keep in mind that if your soul part chooses to switch some of these phases, it is perfectly all right to allow that. You may also find that in some soul retrievals you will skim rapidly through parts of the process while lingering over others, and vice versa. Nevertheless, all phases will be represented in some way or other and in varying time frames.

Emotional Integration

The soul part always integrates fully into your emotions and feelings at the time of the soul retrieval. That is why projection works. The soul part has immediate access to your emotions. That is why you may have instant access to the soul part's strengths and feel dramatically better...or why you do not feel anything because you are used to suppressing your feelings...or why you get more upset than usual over your issues because the soul part relates directly to them. Part of your reaction is due to the soul part's spiritual quality. A dramatic quality like "no nonsense" decisiveness or standing up for yourself is easily noticed. A subtle quality like allowing others to be themselves may be less easy to identify.

How you relate to and use your emotions seems to determine how easy or difficult it is to determine whether the soul part is active within you. As you are open to your feelings, you will allow the soul part to exude its innateness into your feeling nature in regard to its use of its spiritual quality. You will react without thinking, and realize only after the fact that there has been a change in your demeanor or actions.

If you repress your emotions, you will be much less aware of the presence of the soul part at first. If you operate your whole life according to how you feel about events, you may not realize there is any change because you are living totally in the present. Only when others remind you of your change in demeanor, tone, attitude or action, will you begin to recognize cognitively that the soul part is indeed active within you.

Emotional integration is merely the beginning phase and creates only a loose link between you and your soul part. *It does not mean it is fully integrated into all aspects of you.* At this stage, it is entirely possible for the soul part to leave again if you do not work with it.

The First Twenty-Four Hours

After the soul retrieval, usually at least twenty-four hours need to pass before initiating communication with the soul part. The retrieval is like a birthing; if the baby is sleeping, you do not wake it up to find out if it is hungry. You wait for the baby to wake up and then determine what it needs. Likewise, the soul part needs to be the one to initiate communication with you rather than the other way around. It has to get used to being back in physical and to adjust to the new, older person. Often, it likes to sleep for a day or two.

Be like a loving, watchful parent the first twenty-four hours. Do not schedule other activities, if at all possible. Walks in nature are excellent for healing and balancing. If a scheduled activity is necessary, make sure it is something that allows you to focus inward any time the soul part wants your attention. Highly focused, outer-directed activities usually will not allow this.

Be there for the soul part when it initiates communication. Welcome it and listen to it. Ask what it needs and what it wants to say. Then notice any images, memories and thoughts that occur. Interact with it. *Do not discount any experience!* If the communication signal occurs, immediately reflect inward and ask the soul part what it needs or what it wants to say. If emotions arise, allow them. Be loving and bring to mind an image of cuddling the soul part while it expresses its feelings. Notice the thoughts, memories and images that accompany the feelings. Allow it to bring in healing. If it feels right to talk about feelings and memories with someone else, do so.

After twenty-four hours have passed it is all right to initiate contact or do a shamanic journey to the soul part. In trance work, ask spirit helpers for guidance if you are unsure of what needs to happen next.

During the first two weeks after the soul retrieval, keep a diary of *anything new* in your life, no matter how subtle it may seem. This can include new ways of doing things, new attitudes, new ways of looking at the world, others finding something new about you, new abilities, etc. Discount nothing! Do not rationalize it as being due to something else. Recognize that the newness may indeed be partly due to previous work you have done as well as to the soul part now being back; the soul part is helping cement what you have worked on previously. A win-win situation. In other cases, you may find that after a while you will find that the new pattern is because of the soul part or just because you are looking for something new. Some soul parts are dynamic, some subtle. Discounting the subtleties may cause you to ignore or repress a soul part. Such is not wise!

Basic Communication

Basic initial communication involves three facets of healing and attaining rapport between you and your soul part: (1) Rapport with the soul part, (2) Healing yourself and the soul part, (3) Rapport with the soul part's spiritual qualities. This phase is the most crucial yet flexible. They can be done in any order; flowing with the needs of the soul part is paramount.

Rapport with the soul part. The rapport facet involves getting to know the soul part as the sentient being it is; after all, it is you. Not treating it as a person is like treating it as a "thing," and as such, demoralizing for both you and the soul part. Treating the soul part as the person it is, respecting it, valuing it, leads to increasing your self-esteem and self-validation.

In addition, the soul part has specific memories that you may not have, plus an in-depth awareness and mastery of a spiritual quality that you need to experience energetically. It can quickly identify the true source of your issues, transform dysfunctional beliefs, locate and release other people's soul parts attached to you. Treating the soul part as the person it is creates the avenue for an extremely valuable resource that shortens your healing time, strengthens your beauties, and helps to bring about overall self-cohesiveness.

The only distinction between you and the soul part is that it has spiritual qualities different from yours. The nature of its entrusted spiritual quality may require a different form of expression from that to which you are more familiar. It has specific needs and desires that may be foreign to you. Perhaps its form of expression is one that was taboo in your family; if so, you may find it scary.

Hypothetical Case Study *of "Amy."* Amy is quiet and reserved. Yet her soul part is outspoken and assertive because its spiritual quality is the ability to stand up for itself. The family taboo is that outspoken assertiveness is defiance and therefore to be punished. Both the soul part and Amy must work cooperatively with each other, to overcome her fear of speaking out.

During the rapport stage of integration, get reacquainted with the soul part just as you would a long lost friend. Ask what it needs in order to feel completely at home. Let it get to know you as well, noticing how you complement each other and can fulfill each other's needs. Developing a rapport with it helps you integrate it in self-honoring ways that also boost your self-love and self-esteem.

    CASE STUDY of *Diane.* I retrieved two soul parts for Diane. One left when she was a baby and the other left at age eight. For the sake of convenience, we called her soul parts by their ages.

    At her first follow-up session, Diane journeys to the lower world to talk with her soul parts. She inwardly holds her baby soul part, feeling much love for her. The baby knows Diane wants her. Her soul part age eight wants to hold the baby. Diane lets her do so. All three play by the stream in the lower world. The baby plays with rocks from the stream. Diane flies inside the baby's body and observes her from the baby's viewpoint. She notices the feel of the small fat hands. The baby holds up rocks, proud of herself. She is aware of where she is in the moment, and not at all concerned with surroundings. Diane delights in the feel of the baby's body: "It is so pudgy, and uncoordinated!"

Healing yourself and the soul part. The more healing given the soul part before it is brought back, the less healing is needed during the integration process. However, there are times and circumstances that do require further healing at this *Basic Communication* stage. Sometimes the soul part identifies so strongly with a person's issues that it takes on some of that negativity; thus the need for further healing. This healing may take the form of forgiveness of others, circumstances, self and the soul part. The latter may include healing the soul loss causes or forgiving the soul part for leaving. Part of the healing process may be retrieving memories the soul part took with it when it left. Whatever the reason, it is always a good idea to at least ask if the soul part needs more healing. Find out if it notices whether you need that too; both of you may need further healing. Be free with self-honesty and forgiveness.

CASE STUDY of Cara. Cara journeys inward to the lower world to talk with her soul parts (ages two and six) and spirit helpers. I interact with all of them through talking with Cara during the shamanic journey.

Cara: "Two" and "Six", what was the cause of the nasal irritation I experienced this past week?

Two and Six: Criticism was the main factor.

Two: You were self-critical too much and too often. You learned that from your father. It's so automatic that you don't realize it. We wanted you to stop it, but you're not yet ready to hear about the cause of it, the cause from your father.

Maryphyllis: Cara, do you want Two to help you get rid of these automatic, unwanted habits?

Cara: Yes!

Maryphyllis: Let Two get inside your mind and experiences and pitch out the negativity she sees that causes this.

Cara agrees to let Two come inside and do this. Two throws out habits relative to self-criticism, as learned from her father. She starts at the brow chakra, then throat, back of head, under eyes and cheeks. Her legs seem to pulsate, then her lower back solar plexus, buttocks, arms. Finally the energy creates a big wave all along her left side.

(Reader: Notice that Cara experiences all of this at a feeling and body-feeling level. It is not just a mental exercise. The feelings brings the experience firmly into multi-levels of her being, such that there is a transformation of her ordinary reality experience later.)

Maryphyllis: "Ask your power animals and soul parts to bring in healing to fill the spaces vacated by the negativity."

The Deer power animal and soul parts "Two" and "Six" bring in love, to take the place of the dysfunctional patterns. Cara feels energy coming into her heart, then coming off her hips, next a warm spot at the sixth chakra (known as "the third eye"), then upon her head and again to her third eye. Next she feels a pulsing at the bottoms of her feet simultaneously with the third eye, then a slow wave of pulsing energy coming in from her sides, and finally the inside of her knees. Energy enters all of her remembered experiences as well.

Maryphyllis: How can Cara support this process?

Deer, Two, Six: Love yourself, stay in a quiet place with no phone, and be as still as you can. Eat a good meal.

Rapport with the soul part's spiritual qualities. Each soul part carries all or part of a spiritual quality. Although you may already know somewhat what that quality feels like, the soul part may have additional information and a feeling-sense beyond your experience. It is important to feel the quality from the viewpoint of the soul part, and not what you suppose it to be.

Inside the soul part, it is as if *all* of self is that quality. Think about it: When you feel totally loving, the quality of love has full sway over you. When you feel decisive, the decisiveness quality is in the forefront. The soul part has a total focus on one soul quality, to the exclusion of all else. You feel this when you allow it to have full sway of your awareness. The soul part's contribution is what makes the quality feel completely natural.

The compelling importance of this stage of integration is that it helps you feel what it is like to fully enact your soul part's quality. It is more than mere intellectual understanding. Action that *feels* natural is extremely important. Going directly to outer action, without first knowing how it feels inside, may arrest the sense of naturalness. It may even set up conflict between you and your soul part, becoming an "either the soul part's way or my way" situation. It is so much better to have "both-and" cooperation; *that* brings about true integration. If either you or the soul part takes the upper hand, the other side can easily sabotage the effort. Mutual cooperation is vital, to achieve total use of the spiritual quality. Having experienced the soul part's quality in advance, inwardly, you can easily call up the memory of it and the soul part is instantly there, working with you fully. You do not have to struggle to allow the soul part to act in your life, hoping with a "wing and a prayer" that it will work out all right. Knowing how the spiritual quality feels, first hand, creates change more swiftly, more easily, more naturally.

Get to know what spiritual qualities the soul part carries, even beyond what your shamanic practitioner told you it brings. Listen to what the soul part tells you. Then get to know these qualities from *the soul part's viewpoint*. During a journey or hypnotherapy trance, you can more easily attain instant *energetic* knowledge of what the spiritual quality feels like and how the soul part expresses it. Essentially, you just let the soul part take over your feeling nature and sense of self while you inwardly step back and observe, focusing on *feeling the essence* of each quality it shows you. It often will show you some facet of a well-known quality that you did not realize you were missing or that was needed. You also come to know beyond a shadow of doubt that this soul part really knows how to handle the situations it says it does. You can trust it to truly help you in ordinary reality. The exquisite side effect of this process is that it develops self-trust and self-worth to both you and your soul part.

CASE STUDY of Gretchen. At her first follow-up, Gretchen journeys inward to the lower world to talk with her soul parts and spirit helpers. I interact with all of them through talking with Gretchen during the journey.

Maryphyllis: Gretchen, what strengths does your soul bring to you?

Soul Part Age One: Love, power, power to deal with the reality of the world, inner strength, and help with fulfilling your life purpose.

Maryphyllis: Gretchen, would you like to experience these strengths from "One's" perspective? Gretchen does.

Maryphyllis: Confer with her to find out if it's better that you make yourself small and go inside her, or if it is better that she come inside you to convey these strengths to your feeling nature.

"One" goes into Gretchen's heart and womb, then spreads energy throughout her body. She conveys her strengths to Gretchen's feelings. She starts in Gretchen's heart, then produces more lightness in her chest, goes to her lower back, and finally grounds the energy in her feet. "One" releases Gretchen's need to please others. Love and forgiveness come into Gretchen's heart. Anger goes out; light and love come in to replace it.

CASE STUDY of Sheyenne. At her first follow-up session, Sheyenne journeys inward to the lower world to work with her soul parts. I serve as facilitator for the process. The soul parts talk to me through Sheyenne.

Sheyenne says that her soul part Age Eleven looks more "together."

"Eleven" asks Sheyenne, "Are you ready for me?"

Sheyenne: Yes.

Eleven: are you ready to speak my mind?

Sheyenne is unsure what this entails.

Maryphyllis: Sheyenne, do you want to experience what that is like, from her viewpoint?

Sheyenne does, and melts into "Eleven's" body to experience what it is like to speak her mind.

Sheyenne: When I speak my mind, I put myself at risk. I must have strength inside to say, "These are my thoughts and values." There's a big difference in energy. Before, the anger I felt and the amount of energy needed to speak even though I was afraid, was more detrimental to everyone. Eleven's energy is calm and direct, not stressed and tense. There's also a different reaction from people: with Eleven's energy others feel it's OK to listen, hear and respect me. With my former negativity, others were more on guard. But there's still some risk with my boss and even more with my husband. My husband is a mirror to me. He will show me whose energy I'm using: my former style or Eleven's contribution. I will be my husband's teacher in this, as well as discerning my own energy source.

Sheyenne's Guardian Angel: Sheyenne, give Eleven a hug and experience her energy.

Sheyenne does so and sees a blue light. This is calming. Eleven goes into Sheyenne's throat chakra, to stay there for a while.

"Switcheroo." There is a simple yet profound way to learn how to enlist the soul part's help in ordinary reality. When you return from trance, sit up. Close your eyes and envision yourself positioned in the front of your head. Call the soul part to "stand" directly behind you inside your head. Notice how that feels. Then ask the soul part to switch places with you. Notice how that feels. Do this switching several times until you both are comfortable with the veracity of it. Recognizing the difference between who is in front, i.e., in charge, will help you to easily involve the soul part as needed, in your day-to-day events.

Be cognizant of the fact that accomplishing the *Basic Communication Phase* does not mean the soul part is fully integrated and transformed. *If you stay locked into this phase, trouble will escalate.*

Access Total Body And Mind

After energetically experiencing the soul part's spiritual quality, ask the soul part if it wants to insert this new way of being into all your experiences and habits of thought and action. If it agrees, ask it to fill out your entire body, inserting its qualities wherever it deems appropriate.

It will tap into your memories and experiences to discover where to insert its qualities. *You* do not have to know or see all the details. *The soul part* determines the significant events. It may show you how things could have been different had it been here, where you made a good attempt, where further healing needs to be done, give you new uplifting awareness ("aha's") about previous happenings, and what current day activities can be influenced positively by its qualities. If you feel this to be invasive, just remember that it is *you going through you!* And, your spirit helpers can support, guide and nurture you at a moment's notice.

If at any time in the near future you "see" the soul part at a younger age again, do not despair. It does not mean that your previous work has been undone. Rather, it means that the soul part wants to share another of its spiritual qualities, a new aspect of its quality, needs more healing or in some way wants to give you more instruction. Once that is achieved, it will grow back up to your age.

CASE STUDY of Althea. One of Althea's problems that she wanted solved through the soul retrieval was that of over-eating. Eating was a compulsive process; she did not want it. After the retrieval of her two-year-old soul part, Althea no longer had the overwhelming conflict of eat, "beat herself up" about it, eat, "beat herself up". Instead, she ate only when she was hungry. That was different! She also was not depressed at all. In addition, she reported she had an urge to create art with wood.

Althea's integration process contains elements common to a lot of people as well as aspects unique to her. Her story may portray an idea of what happens during the totality of the transformation process.

At her first follow-up session, she journeyed to the lower world and found herself to be a free spirit flying around; this was a metaphor of her new self-image. She had felt her age-two soul part watching her all week. "Two" is "The Watcher." I interact with her, her soul parts and spirit helpers through talking with Althea during the journey.

Althea: "Two", why are you watching me?

(Two does not talk at first. Althea's spirit helper tells her to trust the soul part no matter what. When Althea trusts, Two talks.)

Two: Nothing will ever be the same. No experience will be the same.

Althea: I do not believe that.

Maryphyllis: Althea, do you need details?

Althea: Yes.

Two: Althea has been waiting her whole life for this. It's time. (Althea starts to cry, a joyful cry.) I'm here to take Althea with me, take her back to little girlhood.

Althea laughs: She's showing me how much fun I had; I'd forgotten that. We're sitting in a big tree where I went when I was a child and was scared.

Two: Althea, you did the best you could do – it was ok.

Althea sees Two's face – smiling, for the first time. She knows she does not need to be sad anymore. Two talks to her about her hands, her healing hands. She always had them but never believed it.

Althea: The palms of my hands are burning, a healing-type of burn.

Two: You need to be patient about what you're doing or not doing.

Maryphyllis: Why did Two leave?

Two: Life was not good then, but it is ok now. Althea feels good, and peaceful. She did the best she could do.

Two comes into Althea from the crown of her head, moves down and into her head, and behind her eyes.

Maryphyllis: Althea, do you want to let her go into your experiences?

Althea says yes, so Two does just that.

Two: Grandma is rocking in her rocking chair, and crying. She pats Grandma on the leg and says "It's ok, Grandma." Grandma called Althea "my angel." (This was a new memory that Two gave her. Grandma was about to enter a nursing home and did not want to go.) Althea's heart hurts. She never saw Grandma again, after that

Maryphyllis: Do you need healing?

Althea says yes. She sees a white light that helps her to feel clean, and to let go of the guilt about Grandma and never seeing her again. She rides her horse power animal through the field of the lower world. It feels wonderful and free. As she starts to return from the shamanic journey, she notices that her dolphin power animal is lying on *top* of her return portal. This is new. Blue water appears and she hears the words "go freely." Everything is very clear. The dolphin takes Althea deep under water. Clear water and colored crystals appear to her. Her hands get hot again – a healing energy, such as with crystals. Dolphin tells her to take a course on healing, to learn about her healing hands.

Cleanse Your Aura

A huge barrier to transformation is that of carrying other people's soul parts on you. Those soul parts can interfere with your self-esteem, negate positive thinking, stop you from taking action, keep you locked in dysfunctional attitudes and beliefs, and generally block your attempts at spiritual growth. Before full integration and transformation can happen, these soul parts must be removed. The soul part can identify them more easily than you can; it can see the proverbial forest while you see only the trees.

In trance or a journey, let the *soul part* scan your aura and total being to see if anyone else's soul parts are hanging on you. If so, have your power animals take them off and deliver them to the High Selves of the persons to whom they belong. Do not return them directly to the person because that would be doing an unasked-for healing, which is an ethical "no-no". The person may not be ready for it, and just might send them back to you! In sending the soul parts to their own High Self, that high being will know the right time and circumstance to return it to the person.

If you stay locked in this stage, you still are not fully transformed. The next component is crucial for lasting healing and transformation.

Address Beliefs And Attitudes

We humans tend to adapt easily to life situations. This can be helpful. However, when a soul part goes into soul loss, we adapt without the benefit of all our abilities. This leads to dysfunctional behaviors, such as codependency.

When it leaves, the soul part takes with it its part of a spiritual quality as well as part or all of the memories regarding the soul loss event. In adjusting to the loss, we often develop dysfunctional beliefs and attitudes about self, the nature of life and other people. We also have an incomplete understanding of the departed spiritual quality aspect; this adds to dysfunctional behavior. Dysfunctions become imbedded in the subconscious mind and not available to conscious control.

   Case Study *of "6M".* My "6M" soul part took decisiveness with her when she left at age six-months. I could still make decisions, but the exact moment of decisiveness – when and how to make the decision – escaped me. All I remembered was her intense, pungent adamancy that felt very stern. Therefore, when a difficult decision arose, I tended to use a stern intensity not only to make the decision but also to follow through. I did this even when such an attitude was inappropriate. That intensity could go on for a long time! It was dysfunctional due to my *incomplete* inner information.
   When "6M" returned, she had me feel that intensity for a split second, then returned to peaceful calm throughout the follow-through segment of decision making. She knew how long to use the intensity, whereas "I" did not.

   A crucial component of the transformational process is to look at your false beliefs and transform them into true beliefs, i.e., functional ones. We often "cannot see the forest for the trees" in regard to mistaken beliefs because we are so used to them. They feel "normal." Luckily, the newly returned soul part easily pinpoints discrepancies, what the dysfunction involves, and where and when it occurred. It can also state what the true belief is supposed to be, and help that supplant the dysfunctional one.

   Case Study *of Annabelle.* Annabelle's soul part pointed out the false belief that she should treat others the way she would want to be treated. Annabelle objected, saying, "But this is the Golden Rule!" Her soul part clarified the issue by telling Annabelle that while the Golden Rule may work for others, it actually gets in the way of *her* relationships. Using that rule, she would project her feelings, beliefs and attitudes onto other people; it was the classic mirroring problem. That is, she would read into others' actions something that they were not feeling. In addition, Annabelle was empathic and knew instinctively what others were feeling. Unfortunately, she tended to discount that valuable information. Her soul part "killed two birds with one stone" by rephrasing the belief as: "Treat others the way *they would have* you treat them." Now she uses her intuitive empathy to tell her how the person wants to be treated.

The more the soul part blends with you the more crucial is the need for transforming any dysfunctional beliefs, thought patterns, attitudes and habits you may have. These limiting beliefs are the result of repeated thoughts, affirmations you have said over and over to yourself. Such determine how you treat your soul part, your attitude toward it and the attention you give to it and its strengths. Negating a soul part's quality can make your soul part want to leave again. Even though you want to change, a dysfunctional belief will block any outer action, no matter how hard you try to do otherwise. Beliefs lead to attitudes and habits of thought, which in turn lead to action or blocked action. Change the belief, and you have an easier time changing habits.

Nature abhors a vacuum. If you discard a dysfunctional belief it will only come back again, unless you replace it with a functional one. The soul part's quality is founded in truth; your dysfunctional belief is founded in falsehood. The *soul part* needs to be the one to formulate the functional belief – even down to the exact wording of it.

> **Hypothetical Case Study** of *"Amy."* Amy's dysfunctional belief was that she was not as good as other people. She thought the replacement belief would be "I AM as good as others." Yet her soul part said "I am special and unique. I do not need to be like other people." When Amy heard this and said it aloud, her whole being glowed! The soul part truly "nailed" that issue!

To do this work easily, go on a journey or into trance. Let the *soul part (not "you")* discover if you carry any dysfunctional attitudes or beliefs that would get in the way of its being able to help you fully. If so, have it specify the exact wording; discuss the belief with the soul part until you have a firm understanding that this indeed is a faulty belief. Then ask the soul part to tell you what the replacement wording should be, i.e., giving you a functional belief that will heal your issues and transform your outlook on life. Again discuss it with the soul part until you know beyond a shadow of doubt that the new belief will indeed supplant the old one.

Then ask the *soul part* to cast out the old belief and insert the new belief and ways of being into your experiences and into your subconscious mind. Hold an attitude of unconditional acceptance and allow it to go anywhere it chooses, casting out anything it chooses, even if you do not know the details. Strange as it may seem, all the memories of all your ages are available to it simultaneously. The soul part has such a strong, "single-eyed" focus on its spiritual quality that it instinctively knows where to go within your memories to do this work. It can do the work more quickly if you do not interfere with trying to direct it to specific events. A lot of the work is also at deep pre-verbal levels within the subconscious mind; as you allow it full mobility, it will naturally affect healing at those levels as well.

This process has a side benefit of creating a stronger rapport between you and your soul part. You honor its wisdom and contribution to your life. It, in turn, exudes a glow of self-worth, self-love and self-trust, which you absorb into your total being. You are it; it is you. Win-win!

Occasionally, it is the soul part who is stuck in dysfunctional beliefs. To heal this, let it come inside your mind. But this time it is for the purpose of letting it see the truth of your feelings or beliefs. You need only maintain sincerity and unconditional openness while allowing the soul part to go anywhere it wants to, to check out your veracity. Letting go of control is crucial; the soul part must not get even a glimmer of duplicity from you.

Sometimes a soul part who is stuck in dysfunctional beliefs still does not believe, even though it has thoroughly perused your true beliefs. This is due to disagreement of what is true or important. In this case, find another soul part to talk to it. Make sure Spirit and your other soul parts are the ones to find this other soul part; you must stay out of the selection process, in order to further convey the altruism of your intention. The three of you (you, disbelieving soul part, and believing soul part) then "sit down with each other" in your inner world and discuss the matter. When in doubt as to how to proceed or what to do next, call on your spirit helpers for advice.

Practical Application

All the inner work in the world is to no avail unless you can access the help of the soul part and its spiritual qualities in your everyday life. Take a few weeks to do this. Repeat the inner work as needed.

Remember that the soul part knows more about its spiritual quality than you do. After all, that is why you asked for it to return; you sensed a lack in that area. You can call on it at any time you need its quality. Likewise, respond in kind when it says it is time to put the quality into effect. If the soul part tells you what action you need to take, do it. If you are apprehensive, ask the soul part to take action for you. If the action fails, ask the soul part and your spirit helpers for a solution, during a trance state or journey.

This inner work is for healing and rapport. The reality of it proves itself in ordinary reality. The returned soul part knows how and when to act. Expect it to take action. Whether this action is positive or negative depends upon how thoroughly you and your soul part are healed. When you take positive action, you work *with* the soul part's quality. If you take negative action or no action at all, the soul part *will* get its way: through projection, resistance, negative emotions, sabotage, or even depression.

Soul parts often reveal more qualities or aspects of qualities, and need more healing later. To avoid problems, honor their new input.

If you stay locked in this phase, especially without inner work, trouble will escalate.

Permanent Adulthood

The soul part may grow up to your age and then in a subsequent journey it shows up young once again. If this happens, do not despair; the previous growth has not been trashed. Its change in age merely signifies that it has something more to discuss with you or to be healed further.

Once it remains your age, permanently, it is saying that all issues have been settled and both of you are compatible. *But this does not mean it is fully integrated nor that you both are transformed.*

CASE STUDY of Althea. Session two, two weeks after the first transformation session. Althea now feels the best ever. This week she did numerous journeys on her own, to her soul part. "Two" is grown up to thirty-one. When Two reached age twenty-one, Althea bought a bike, on Two's impulse and set up an exercise program; this was something she never would have done previously. She still has burning hands, indicative of healing ability, and a motivation to heal others.

She journeys inward to the lower world to talk with her soul parts and spirit helpers and I interact with them through her, as we did in the first session.

Two: "Go forward! Trust this is what's happening." She leads Althea down a long path and says, "You need to trust yourself."

Power animals surround Althea. They say she needs to remember them; they will give her strength, clarity and power. Two embraces Althea. It is a powerful feeling, a floating feeling. She is now in a circle of power animals. Her spirit teacher sits next to Two and says, "Look into the campfire." Althea sees a huge purple crystal, a stone of healing. She sees her face in it. She feels warm inside, vibrating, when she touches the smooth stone. The power is in her hands; her spirit teacher touches them.

Althea rides her horse power animal fast, to try to cool her hands. But it will not work; the heat will not go away. Dolphin is in her face and says, "The heat isn't going to go away." They go back to the campfire circle. Two has now grown up to age forty, and has gray hair. She smiles, happily. She talks about being worthy and says, "Trust, believe." The crystals in front of her remind Althea to believe. They are energy, like teardrops. The bear power animal stands over Althea and gives her strength. She sits in the middle of the circle of power animals, with Two and her spirit teacher. She is told, "Our shamanic journey is protected."

Suddenly, Althea sees Althea (!) sitting across from her. That feels strange! Yet good. Althea, who used to be soul part age Two, flies overtop the circle. Althea is in Althea's face. Now they are as one and she sits down. She is totally relieved of doubt, has total trust, and feels centered. She is fully integrated and transformed.

Massive Blending

A soul part that is grown up to your current age has access to all your experiences and can enact its quality in your life. But if you still feel its presence as separate from you, and have to enlist its help, consciously, it is not fully transformed within you. You may be able to work cooperatively with it, but it is not totally one with your being. At this point, several aspects finish the process.

They are not mental meandering exercises. Rather, they involve inner energetic blending, which you may or may not experience at the feeling and body energy levels like Cara experienced, as mentioned earlier in the chapter. These several processes are as follows:

"Staying" and "Leaving" Powers. Each of us has a "staying" quality, i.e., a trait that has kept us in body while the rest of our soul fled. Much of psychotherapy is predicated on clients developing "staying power" with process, toughing it out and progressing safely, which they interpret as going slowly. That is necessary and indeed safe, because they usually work with the person-who-has-stayed-in-body. Therapists who work with a person who suffered trauma are working with someone who has this staying quality. Therefore they can help the person "go slowly" and not access memories too fast to handle safely.

This applies to many retrieved soul parts as well: Ones who left inadvertently or left in order to make life easier for us. For example, a soul part that carries deep wisdom may not be accepted in the family because its parents believe that a very small child has no business telling them what to do and what is wise. Therefore the soul part entrusted with the "wisdom" aspect chooses to leave in order for the child to behave in a more harmonious way with its family. "Wisdom's" altruism will probably allow it to readily take on the person's staying power when it is retrieved.

"Leaving" Power. The above is *not* the case when working with other returned soul parts. Many soul parts who leave voluntarily *probably* do not have the staying-quality. They left once before because they were not about to put up with life circumstances. If the therapy goes slowly or if their needs are not attended to immediately, they will create all kinds of emotional havoc. They may stir up emotions and attitudes, causing personal and relationship problems, or refuse to allow the spiritual quality to manifest, or leave again in soul loss. They will bring up memories when *they* are ready, not when you or the therapist is. For them, progressing faster, i.e., frequent action, in the healing work is safer than going slowly. For these reasons also, the returning soul part needs to link, energetically and willingly, with your staying quality at some point in the process. In fact, there is no harm in asking all soul parts – ones who left and ones who stayed – to link with the staying quality. This serves to blend them more fully within the totality of you.

To do this, the soul part needs to merge with or take part of the "staying quality" that kept you in body while all those other soul parts left. Reflect on what those qualities are that kept you here. Each person's "list" is different, so trust what comes to your mind. Then in a trance state or journey, ask the soul part to take part of that and mix it with the qualities it brings you. Doing this it meshes with the rest of you in a way that is so intertwined that you know it will never want to leave again in this life or any other. Its staying power is strengthened.

Etheric Web Blending. The etheric web is the first layer of the aura and is the blue-print for the physical body. Your hand could be cut off, yet a special photo of your aura would show it to be still there. After this phase is complete, you have full, unconditional, innate, immediate use of the soul part's intelligent guidance and spiritual quality. It is only here that you can be assured that the soul part will never leave again.

When the soul part blends into the "Web", it may feel energetically like "furniture rearranging," or like "dye infusing into water," or pure energy pulsing throughout the body that convey total unity. Some people inwardly see this happening, or just know that it is. The following are several ways in which to achieve this phase.

(1) **Spontaneously**. Without instruction and without warning, your soul part or your spirit helpers may automatically lead you into this blending phase....much like what happened with Althea in the case study above. Your experience may or may not resemble instances illustrated in this book, yet you will know that the blending is indeed happening.

(2) **High Self Blending**. A second way is through the use of your High Self. In a journey or trance state, ask your High Self to shine its powerful healing light all around and through you. Ask your soul part to let the High Self move it to wherever in your being the High Self knows the soul part is supposed to be. Then let it happen. The energy may feel like it is coursing through you or that is "furniture rearranging." Probably the High Self is involved in the spontaneous ways also (#1 above).

(3) **Etheric Web Blending**. This style is more involved and is more easily done within a shamanic Journey. From the description, you may find it easy to ask your High Self to complete the process if you choose the High Self Blending form. Whichever you choose, be sure to allow the process to unfold *energetically* rather than letting your mind meander. If you are unsure of your

ability it is probably better to work with a facilitator such as a spiritual hypnotherapist or a shamanic practitioner.

(a) Ask your High Self to show you what your Etheric Web looks like. People have reported fish net, spider web, hanging white basket, swirling colors, a grid. Go with what the High Self shows you.

(b) Ask your soul part to position itself within that web wherever it knows it is. What it shows you may surprise you. You know it grew up to your age and filled out your whole body. Even though it may have access to your whole body, it may well prefer to be in just one place. Accept what it shows you.

(c) Ask your High Self to shine its powerful healing light all around and through the web. Ask your soul part to let the High Self move it to wherever in your being the High Self knows the soul part is supposed to be. Then let it happen, and notice what you see or feel.

(d) Ask the High Self to clean out all strands of the web. This may look or feel like a deep inner cleansing; it makes sure nothing contaminates the next few stages.

(e) Ask the soul part to connect into the web, like it is an open "phone line" to all parts of you.

Core Of Your Being

The core of your being carries the beliefs, attitudes and the very essence of who you consider yourself to be. Ideally, only the purest and most uplifting values, beliefs and traits should occupy this area. However, it is possible to store here other people's soul parts and any beliefs about yourself and life that are damaging.

Along with the Massive Blending, the soul part needs to merge with the absolute core of your being, wherever you perceive that to be within or around your body; your heart, solar plexus, head, aura? Doing this, the soul part takes on or melts into the core of who you are and you take on its full awareness of self. This stage requires absolute self-trust that the total awareness will work out well. By the time all of the healing, clearing and rapport work have been completed, perhaps trust is a "given." As Althea described, "We are now as one."

Be mindful, however, that this stage must not occur until all the healing and your access to the soul part's qualities is complete. If you go to this stage too early, the soul part may reject going into the core – *which is healthy!* Rejoice in its wisdom. It knows that if it goes in before it is completely healed, it brings its unhealed negativity deep inside you, linking that with who you know you are. That would be insidious. You would begin identifying yourself partly with the negative aspects rather than totally with the positive traits. It would then become very hard to heal because you would not think you could part with what you believe to be you!

Usually the soul part knows when it is appropriate and safe to go into the core of your being. When it does choose to merge with you there, take a few moments to feel the *essence* of you, with it there.

Then ask the soul part to look around and see if there is anything that should not be there, such as dark or foggy places, someone else's soul parts, dysfunctional beliefs or attitudes. If so, have your spirit helpers remove and transmute the dark or foggy stuff or take the soul parts to their own High Selves, or ask the soul part to help you change the dysfunctional beliefs and attitudes to functional ones. When that is complete, again take a few moments to feel what the pristine condition of the core of your being is like.

Then ask the soul part to totally fuse into you so that the two of you become one.

Transformation is now complete
for that soul part and its qualities within you

Note: Clearing the core of your being can be done any time, whether in connection to a soul retrieval transformation process or not. Your spirit helpers would then be the ones to identify anything that needs to go or be transformed.

Even if you do this work ahead of receiving a soul retrieval, it is still a good idea to have your soul parts check for anything that should not be there. Each soul part has its own special "lens" of perception that can see things no other soul part and no spirit helper can see. What is visible to one is invisible to another.

Complicated?

All this may sound complicated and time consuming, but some people have been known to achieve all these phases within the first week after the soul retrieval. A lot depends upon the soul part, its reason for leaving, the quality it brings you, how much you have been able to work on the issue ahead of time, and you. Each soul part transforms differently. You react differently according to the issue addressed by the soul retrieval.

Anchoring The Healing

After each stage of transformation, it is helpful to anchor the healing and new ways of being into your subconscious and every molecule of your being. While this can be done in many different ways, here is what I do: Ask your High Self to bring its powerful healing and purifying light down around and through you. Then ask it to take all the healing and new strengths of the session into every molecule of your being, physical and non-physical, to help you adapt easily to the changes. As it does this, allow it to go anywhere it needs to whether you know that location or not, and whether you feel it or not. This is an energetic experience, not intellectual meandering. Hold yourself open, trusting and completely surrendering to Spirit and your subconscious that it will happen.

When that seems complete, ask High Self also to take the healing and new strengths into your "Command Pathways." These are areas within the subconscious mind that send the command to your conscious mind to be, act and feel in certain innate ways. None of us have to deliberate about awareness of self and life; it just is. And that is what you want for these new strengths and healing: instantaneous adaptation.

The command comes from the core of your being, deep within the subconscious mind. In order to get to that indefinable place within, you do not need to know exactly where it is. It is an instinctive place your subconscious knows, the place that commands you to be as you are, instinctively. Ask your High Self to take the healing and new strengths into your Command Pathway Levels, much like it did with the "molecules of your being".

As you go through your daily life, you may encounter differing results of this "anchoring" work. Sometimes you may find yourself automatically acting and thinking in the new way; when you realize such, thank yourself and Spirit for their help. At times you may find your mind giving you a choice: new way or old way? Then choose the new way and again thank yourself and Spirit for their help. Then, on occasion, if you find yourself thinking or acting in the old way, stop and affirm that the next time you will choose the new way. As you affirm, thank Spirit and yourself for making this choice. There is no distinction among these differing choices your subconscious will give you, although the last one may indicate your need to do further healing regarding the situation. This is especially true if you continue to fall back into the old way of being.

Transformation Over-View

To help heal, integrate and transform a soul part, the following needs to happen, although not necessarily in the order shown here:

- Attentiveness to the soul part;
- Awareness of communication from the soul part;
- Both you and the soul part achieve healing and release of negative emotions stemming from the soul loss incident;
- Discovering spiritual qualities the soul part brings;
- Experiencing these qualities from the soul part's view;
- Discovering ways the soul part will help improve your life;
- Actively applying the soul part's spiritual qualities in life;
- You and the soul part co-operate so that there is mutual respect and access to all abilities;
- Stretching the soul part into all areas of your body;
- Growing the soul part up to your current age, healing and explaining events as it requests such;
- Letting the soul part access all your memories and experiences, as *it* deems pertinent;
- Healing aspects of yourself that may block the soul part from fully healing and transforming;
- Transforming dysfunctional beliefs, attitudes and habits of thought and action;
- Letting the soul part's qualities merge with other spiritual qualities as the *soul part sees is appropriate;*
- The soul part is permanently grown up to your age;
- Letting the soul part link into your etheric web and High Self for full access to spiritual healing, spiritual attunement and knowing yourself more fully;
- The soul part merges with the core of your being, wherever you perceive that to be;
- The soul part identifies anything in the core that is not supposed to be there, and your spirit helpers aid removal and/or changes;
- The soul part blends into you like "dye in water" and becomes one with you.

Desired End-Results

In most cases, and with faithful work on your part, the following desired results should occur within one month of the soul retrieval. Core soul parts, that need to retrieve and link with other soul parts, may take longer.

 • The soul part is permanently grown up to your age and fully one with you;
 • You have full innate use of all of your spiritual qualities, with no negative side effects;
 • The issues addressed by the soul retrieval are healed.

The over-view and end-results listings above rarely occur in one session, although they can. If you try to attain all of this too early in the work, you may sabotage the transformation process. That is because you could inadvertently by-pass details that the soul part deems necessary. You could also be manipulating yourself in a blatantly disrespectful way. Cooperation between you and the soul part is paramount for full transformation. Your soul part is not supposed to rule over you any more than you are to rule over it. For full healthy healing, cultivate open expression and honesty of feeling within you.

Spirit's design for us humans
is to be more than merely a collection of aspects and qualities.
Rather, Spirit intends for us
to be a fully transformed, blended whole.

CHAPTER 7

OTHER WAYS TO TRANSFORM YOUR SOUL

The Inner Mind

Ingrained beliefs, attitudes and habits are lodged in the subconscious mind. If you know what they are, you can access them consciously and therefore have control over their action in your life. Anything you cannot access you have no control over. Outer stimuli can "push your buttons" and you momentarily act on automatic impulse, whether desirable or undesirable. For instance, walking ability is an automatic action requiring nothing more than the desire to do it. Its automatic impulse is desirable, while mindless response to "button pushing" is not. When there has been soul loss, dysfunctional coping mechanisms that allow the "button-pushing" mode develop within the subconscious mind.

For many people, working solely with "mindful awareness of the soul part" allows the mind to catch only the most obvious communication signals from the soul part. You miss the subtle levels. This is because the mind stays at the rapid thinking level (called beta brainwave) used for decision-making. Deeper more relaxed levels of the mind must be accessed in order to become aware of subtler communications. These subtle signals are the most significant for full interweaving of the self, because they are connected to beliefs and to Spirit. A metaphor of this level of thought is that of riding in an airplane: you can see the whole vista for hundreds of miles. You can see where the grass is, but cannot see the individual blades of grass nor a ring you may have lost there.

Even the most experienced "inner-travelers" benefit from subtle work in the deeper levels of the mind. These deeper levels speed up the process of transformation and are found in shamanic journeying, hypnotherapy and guided imagery. Deeper levels of the mind bring through a strong sense of truth. When the soul part says something, you know it is true and that you are not making it up. A metaphor for this deep level is that of walking over the same terrain you saw earlier from the plane. You cannot see for hundreds of miles around, but you are still aware of what is there. Now you can see each individual blade of grass and the lost ring that was there all along. In other words, accessing deeper levels of the mind allows you to see what has really been there, active in your life, all along.

To work only within the surface perimeters of the conscious mind is like looking for a lost coin in a well- lit room even though you know it rolled down the steps to a dark basement. If you want to find that precious coin, you have to go to the basement to where it actually is!

Guided imagery, hypnotherapy and shamanic journeying help you access the deeper levels of your personal basement, i.e., the inner storehouse of the subconscious and spiritual minds. This deeper state is called "trance." It is an intensely alert state of mind that also taps into a spiritual calm that allows you to move beyond your conscious mind's defense system and connect with the subconscious, the High Self and your soul's purpose. Here is where you have the strong resource of spirit helpers to heal and support you. The process is gentle, easier to fathom, and produces more lasting results.

Trance work facilitates lasting healing, truer communication with the soul part and its connection to you. You can recognize subtleties that would otherwise escape surface awareness, just as when you are walking you can see the individual blades of grass that were not discernible from the sky. Within trance, it is much more *obvious* that a soul part is talking to you and not just a "figment of the imagination." Tapping into your feelings or that inner calmness, you know you are not making it up. You discover the unique way in which the soul part communicates so you can more easily be mindful of the soul part in ordinary reality.

Ritual

Ritual, in and of itself, may not be sufficient for inner communion with the soul part. As in the Lakota Sun Dance, which is preceded by an intensely focused yearlong period of prayer and purification, the dance itself is the *end result* of a lot of forethought, preparation and genuine sincerity. Participants say that it is not the ritual that transforms. Rather, it is all the inner work leading up to it that does so.

When Ritual Works. Ritual for soul transformation tries to approximate how the process is done in tribal cultures. There, the tribe has an intrinsic unified awareness of the inner spirit of the ritual. The ritual therefore easily reaches into each person's inner mind. In the case of the Lakota Sun Dance, tribe members watching the Sun Dance are spiritually uplifted, affected by the profoundly spiritual atmosphere of the ceremony.

Some people have a gift of being able to go into trance while moving; for example, Sufi Dervishes, Native American dancers, body workers, gifted athletes, and emotionally expressive painters. They say they are "in the zone" and can even meditate while moving. There are also some people who are very sensitive to their inner process, are able to go into trance at will, do not repress their feelings, and have a soul part whose nature is outwardly or emotionally expressive. All of these people may discover that outer ritual is a highly effective means for integrating soul retrievals. That is, they could well experience intense inner communication even while outwardly moving. The movement, as well as the intent of the ritual, produce the trance state necessary for communicating with the soul part. For these people, ritual is needed.

When Ritual Does Not Work. This uplifting experience may or may not occur in our industrial society. Even within a specific church's spiritual family there may be a diversity of spiritual and personal beliefs. Each person does not necessarily embrace another's supernatural understanding in the same way. A meaningful ritual to one person is an empty ritual to someone else.

Where one person merges easily with the ritual, another person may feel very self-conscious. Where one can let a song move their spirit, another finds singing distracting. To those for whom movement gets in the way of inner communication, physical ritual is not helpful. Outer physical ritual and light meditation may not be able to move them into the deep state of awareness needed to pick up on the subtle signals from the soul part. Or, when they do try to listen, they feel like they are making it all up. That is what light trance (called alpha brainwave) feels like: "it is just our imagination" making it up. So when the soul part tries to communicate, they think it is not real, i.e., they are fabricating the experience. Or they may literally not be able to hear the soul part.

Outer ritual exercises address only the "tip of the iceberg" for these people. Ritual can create a sense that the integration is complete when it really may not be. It can also convey a sense that nothing happened at the soul retrieval. Either way, the ritual may create future problems, needlessly, because you think you no longer need to try to contact the soul part. If you experience any negative projection, escalation of your issues, or turbulent emotions regarding these issues, then in all probability it is coming from your soul part. The soul part is trying to get its needs met and expresses pain because of your lack of attention to it, its healing and your unfinished transformation.

Life-Application

The ultimate desired outcome in soul transformation is to have full use of the soul energy, awareness, intelligence, and the spiritual qualities along with the full blending of the soul's sense of self with your sense of self. All of this must be without the hampering influence of negative energies, emotions and beliefs. All of this should be available to you round-the-clock.

The inner work proposed in this book forms the background healing that allows you to apply the soul part's qualities in your life. After each session of inner work it is very important that you actively apply in your everyday life the strengths you healed and gained during the session. This tests its effectiveness. You know the healing work is complete when life-application is easy, natural and lasting. You know you have more inner work to do when you find life-application difficult. Commit to life-application and you will honor your soul part as well as building your self-esteem.

Trance Work

Shamanic Journeying as a vehicle for transformation is self-empowering and gentle. It is self-empowering because you can do it without another human facilitating it. It is gentle because within the journey you are held in unconditional acceptance and love, and you are not given more than you can handle. You have direct contact with your spirit helpers for healing and advice at any time you choose to journey. Spirit can reach into the subconscious and bring about healing and change swiftly and gently. There is no pain. All you feel are the beneficial effects from it. Then in ordinary reality you notice an easy, natural change in how you feel, think and act.

Other Ways To Transform Your Soul

Sometimes people are nervous about doing journeying and wonder if there may be some other way of accomplishing the same ends. Usually that is just "performance anxiety" or "fear of failure" talking. As you follow through with the process, you will find that you can indeed achieve the deep levels of trance necessary for successful journeying. I am sure you will be delightfully awed at the result. Many is the time that people who have a difficult time meditating are able to journey.

If you have any concern, however, it probably would be better for you to learn journeying during a private session. That way, your shamanic practitioner can step in at a moment's notice to help if you show signs of thwarting your success.

Spiritual Hypnotherapy. Hypnotherapy originated from shamanic journeying. Both require a deep state of trance. There are two primary differences between them, though: (1) Journeying can be done alone, whereas hypnotherapy nearly always requires a facilitator for your process. This means that all of your inner healing has to be done in session, with only life-application occurring on your own. (2) Hypnotherapy is done solely in middle world, while journeying for soul transformation is done in upper or lower world. The latter is much deeper and has as well a spiritual essence that enhances your experience.

In journeying, you always have access to your true spirit guides to both guide and heal you at a moment's notice. *Spiritual* hypnotherapy includes the use of spirit guides or an archetypal being that represents your inner wisdom. Some people know their guide is real; later they find they can access it for guidance in various events of life. Other people question the veracity of this inner wisdom source and do not often access it outside of the session.

Nevertheless, spiritual hypnotherapy is a valuable resource for bringing about soul transformation. The depth of alert trance brings you into contact with a sense of truth of experience. You *know* it is your soul part you are conversing with; the interaction does not feel imaginary. For healing, I always have you call in your High Self; this being is capable of high-powered healing at any time you call on it.

ALTERNATE METHODS

Spirit designed the methods of this book to be used during a shamanic journey or spiritual hypnotherapy. In some cases it may be possible to use these while in lighter states of trance such as meditation or energy work. I have done that at times, for myself and for a few clients who were unable to do journeying or hypnotherapy. I have not felt them to be quite as effective as deeper states, but maybe you will find a way to do that.

As a general guideline, I am including in this chapter what I have noticed about those alternative methods of transformation. If you find new ways to implement them effectively, bravo! And please share them with me, especially any principles of application that go beyond what I describe here.

Energy Healing only, for integration. Body workers, dancers and others whose attention is primarily of the energetic-knowledge mode may find this form very helpful. It is also helpful for those who cannot maintain an alert trance state, and for those whose rational mind will not release control of the creative and feeling levels of mind. *Benefits for those who are body-oriented:* Images arise and changes occur easily, if you are aware of your body's way of communicating soul knowledge. Clear communication and integration occur with your soul part even without the intervention of someone else's energy healing. *Benefits for those who are not body-oriented:* Uplifting feeling of the energy work and the luxury of someone else doing it all for you. Images may arise and changes may occur easily. It would be especially helpful if the energy worker obtains and shares intuitive or channeled information with you regarding the soul part and its qualities. Insist that your healer make a tape-recording of your session so that you can review information later, and act on it in ordinary reality. *Pitfalls:* You may or may not have rapport with your soul part and could treat it like a "thing." If this is true, you will encounter the same pitfalls as the "orphan," as it was described earlier in this book. It is imperative to work with the soul part in ordinary reality.

"Tip of the Iceberg" includes meditation, ordinary reality ritual, alert "mindfulness" of the soul part in ordinary reality." Some soul parts integrate and transform well with these methods. People who have had little soul loss and have a strong background in inner work also may transform well with these methods. Many do not, however. They may take many months or years to fully integrate and transform, if at all. There is a better chance of these styles being effective *after* first doing inner healing.

Meditation: If your style of meditation allows information to arise to awareness, you may be able to communicate with the soul part. In this case, follow instructions under the "Dye In Water" section, to affect full transformation.

Ordinary Reality Ritual: You may have an easy time with this style if you flow easily with energy work or get information in meditation or find that ritual takes you into a trance state. If none of these apply, you would be better off with a facilitated trance state to first get the healing and rapport needed. Then, in ordinary reality, do the ritual to cement the inner healing.

Mindfulness: Being constantly mindful for signals and communication from the soul part is a necessary part of *all* forms of integration and transformation. The signal is a reminder to nurture it, listen to it, and allow its strengths to blossom into activity. This form of work is helpful if you are well versed in inner work and know yourself very well. If such is not the case, you would be better off to use it only after the inner healing has been done. This is because, in ordinary reality, it is easy to dismiss thoughts and emotions as something you have always experienced, rather than being actual communication from the soul part. Mindfulness is usually not deep enough to affect full healing. **Pitfalls:** If you are not able to be constantly attentive, the soul part's energy will only magnify your faults and issues. Improvement is short-lived. Fears, subtleties, and unhealed soul loss incidents lead to inner conflict and relationship havoc.

"Latch-Key Child." *Conventional talk therapy and working on issues alone.* Some people and some soul parts need this form of work. However, it is not fruitful if issues work circumvents the soul part and focuses only on symptoms. In addition, this form of work usually requires much external guidance and intervention, as occurs within the counseling session. As a result, it might take a year or more to evidence full benefit from the soul retrieval, if at all. **Benefits:** You pay attention to yourself and make progress in areas not relating to soul loss. Some soul parts integrate well with issues work *plus* mindfulness.

Suggested Option: Ask your therapist to read this book and use it to work with the soul part. That is, your therapist should speak directly to your soul part rather than treating it as a "thing", go straight to the incidents and specific issues relating to the soul loss to heal them, help you discover the spiritual qualities and focus on blossoming them, help you transform dysfunctional attitudes and beliefs to functional ones, and pay close attention to projection. Then obtain help from a hypnotherapist to attain the final stages of work. *Pitfalls:* You treat the soul part as a thing, not as the person you and it are. If you do not go straight to the incidents and specific issues relating to the soul loss, the soul part will magnify dysfunctional attitudes and behavior, emotionally scream about conflicting beliefs, project issues onto others, and cause havoc in relationships.

"Chocolate Milk Mixing." *Trance work such as shamanic journeying, guided imagery and spiritual hypnotherapy.* These forms help you communicate with the soul part directly, hopefully with the aid of your spirit helpers. Healing is deep and more permanent. You can more easily access the soul part and its quality during ordinary reality life. *Benefits:* In spiritual dimensions, the integration/transformation work is gentle, deeply supportive, self-honoring and not emotionally painful. You glean deeper insight, subtle details and a sense of reality in the soul part's communication. *Pitfalls:* You must take time for yourself. If you do not combine this form of work with Mindfulness, improvement will be short-lived, much like chocolate separating from milk. You may have to always work at accessing the soul part in ordinary reality; access is not automatic. In other words, this style of work stops short of full transformation.

"Dye In Water." *Insights and unique methods Spirit has given me, as contained in this book* help you complete and go beyond the "Chocolate Milk Mixing" style above.

Spontaneous Soul Retrieval. If the soul part returns spontaneously and is constructively integrated into all aspects of your life, then perhaps you have done all the inner healing work that is needed for its safe return. *Benefits:* Ask your spirit helpers if the soul part is fully healed. If so, you can safely invite it into you. You will have full access to the soul part's qualities at all times, without the resistance of unhealed issues. There will be no projection in those healed areas. *Pitfalls:* If your spirit helpers have any reservations about the status of the soul part's healing, *do not invite it into your being!* Leave it there in the inner world! If you invite it into you prematurely, you will take on its unhealed energy, turbulent emotions and negative attitudes. That will cause havoc in your life and relationships. Seek help from a shamanic practitioner or spiritual hypnotherapist to help you heal the soul part and commence with the process advocated in this book.

Even when you feel that the soul part has been fully healed and accesses all levels of your being, keep a watchful eye on it for a while. If you experience problems with your emotions, attitudes and/or behavior, seek a proper professional to help you heal.

CHAPTER 8

EPILOGUE: LASTING EFFECTS?

Now that you have gleaned an idea of what to expect during the soul retrieval and its transformation process, it would be important to know how lasting the work is. Of course, this varies from person to person according to what aspect of life they were working on with the soul retrieval. Those who addressed a life-long, even all-lives-long, issue found a need to continue their work using other modalities in addition to fairly frequent soul retrievals. Those who addressed an issue that wasn't a core issue, found immediate and long-lasting results with their soul retrieval and its transformation.

This chapter reveals brief accounts of some of my clients; the names given are aliases, in order to preserve their anonymity. Each person has reported on the reason for their soul retrieval, how they felt immediately after the transformation process was complete, and how all of this has lasted years later.

Clients Whose Stories Appeared Earlier In This Book

Hera (Chapter 4) had the interior walls of her house painted five years after her soul retrieval in 1995. The paint fumes presented no problem to her because she could stay at her mother's house while the paint fully dried. In two weeks she was comfortable returning to her house. In 2007, she could tolerate a room that had been painted several days previously. She does not necessarily like the smell, but it has no detrimental effect on her.

Maia (Chapter 4) continued to be comfortable speaking up in groups larger than four, even up until her death in 1996.

Karen (Chapter 5) received her soul retrieval in 1999. She said, "I came to the soul retrieval because I had a vision, while I was driving, that I had died and that my inner child was leaning over me crying and begging me not to die. To say the least, I pulled the car over and sat there for almost an hour unable to stop sobbing. I put it together that I was dying on a soul level and that is when I searched you out.

"Strangely enough, much of my retrieval processing involved grieving for the little girl and recognizing the strengths of the adult. I had grown up in a Catholic family of intuitives, but that ability had always been labeled as "crazy" so I learned early on to squash all of that. I had a horrible reaction to the vision of a witch that appeared in one of our sessions and also the snake, which turned out to be my power animal. I was so taken back by the witch that I almost stopped seeing you. Later, my response from the sessions was to embrace the witch as symbolizing all of my wonderful intuitive and healing energy that was part of that vibration. The snake became colorful and laughing as my creative gifts came back.

"My abilities have grown day by day to the point that I have been asked many times to work as a medical intuitive. Case in point, I had a friend several years ago who was diagnosed with cancer and was working with Duke Hospital for healing. They had given him six months to live. Two years later they came out to his home to interview him regarding what he was doing to have lived that long. He explained to them that it was because of all of the healing energy work that I did on him.

"There was a little part of me that became fearful again as that seemed to be too much knowledge for the general public to know (witch burnings!) but once again I came to you and you did my healing work from long distance. That session glued all of my parts together and I have felt totally whole since that time.

"I no longer have fear of any of my gifts. I welcome them whenever I discover them. I have also developed a sense of peace that is almost difficult to imagine would ever exist. I used to say years ago that I always felt like there was a reservoir in me that sometimes got completely empty and I lived many days with a huge empty hole inside of me. I am always full now. I may be tired, but I am never empty or the least bit drained in my reservoir. I welcome my gifts, I don't fear any reactions that they might bring and I laugh a lot. That is what your work did for me!!"

Sophie *(Chapter 5)* said, "Prior to my soul retrieval in 1998, I had an ineffective pattern of standing up for myself. I voiced my truth with a meek, gentle tone of voice, rather than from a place of authority. Unfortunately, others took this to be weak or that I didn't really mean it. Some even thought I was trying to manipulate them and they didn't like that. From the soul transformation process, I realized that my "Caring" soul part was trying to take over the job of assertive parts that were missing, and was doing a poor job of it. Those new assertive parts are back, taking over their rightful duties; they give me a stronger, truer voice when I stand up for myself. Nine years later, there are still times I slip back into the former dysfunctional way, and that is when I feel intimidated. But even so, when I realize what's happening, I know how to change that around. It is now much easier to do, through refocusing my attention, posture and voice."

Lynne (Chapter 5) said, "Maryphyllis, your work has been very beneficial on my path as a healer. The work we did six years ago has remained healed. Of course new things come up, but I know how to clear them and move forward. I still use a lot of what you taught me, too. My medicine bag needs a wagon!

"I have continued learning and expanding my shamanic and traditional healing studies and have helped many people. I receive exciting testimonials that remind me of the one I sent to you six years ago. These people go on to help others and they help others and so on; it keeps getting paid forward, to come back to you in bountiful blessings. It is so wonderful for healers to support and help each other. There is much work to be done and the more we spread the light and the love, the more we heal the world. Imagine a world without emotional pain, people working together and honoring all life on our planet. This is what we are growing, Maryphyllis; let's keep planting those seeds of light."

Annabelle (Chapter 6) said that her new belief and intention worked well for a while, after completing the transformation process. She could automatically sense how someone wanted to be treated, and complied accordingly. Then she started taking that sensing a bit too far. That is, a few of her close friends commented on her energy being uncomfortably invasive. At that point, she called me for another short session. This was in 2004.

During the session, she realized that there was an even deeper belief in operation: she felt the only way she could get information about the other person was to sense their emotional and feeling environment. I asked her what her spirit helpers wanted to say about that. They told her to consult them and her High Self for advice in situations she was not sure she could handle. In some instances she was just to consult her own conscience regarding appropriate actions and words.

In 2007 she was feeling a lot more confident in situations where she could communicate with people face to face or over the phone. She still had an uncomfortable feeling about emails and hand-written letters, though.

Cara (Chapter 6) said, "My life-long issue has been that of learning about love in all its varieties and complexities. This includes love towards myself as well as from others. In my current life, my biggest stumbling blocks have all pointed back to my relationship with my parents. No matter what I did or said, they never quite "got" how their actions and words hurt me.

"The forgiveness ritual, which was part of and in addition to other facets of the transformation process, has had a profound effect on my relationship with my parents. I did many forgiveness rituals involving them. As the cording was released and the holes healed, it became evident that they really did receive the healings as well, even though they didn't consciously know I was doing that.

"My father was able to let go of always needing to be right and to doing-it-his-way. This earlier dynamic greatly stifled the development of my creativity and confidence in my abilities. We can now discuss how to do a task or project. It is much more enjoyable working with him.

"My mother was finally able to stop criticizing me about my weight and appearance. There were a couple of times throughout the years when she would start in on me again, but I was finally able to ask her to stop and to relay how much her words hurt my feelings. She can now say supportive words rather than criticism."

Diane (Chapter 6) has been doing shamanic healing and soul retrieval work for others over the past ten years. She feels a lot more confident and self-sufficient.

Sheyenne (Chapter 6) came to me with a concern about not being able to meditate and to feel a connection to Spirit. The soul retrieval gave her that connection. She completed her transformation work within two follow-up sessions. About a month after that, she reported having a much easier time with meditation, as well as a more constructive relationship with authority figures! Recently, now about ten years later, she told

Epilogue: Lasting Effects?

me that she still has a good meditation practice and connection to Spirit.

Althea (Chapter 6) said that her soul retrieval and transformation process was extremely profound in its life-changing effects. Improved self-image, sense of freedom, and enjoyment of life were part of this.

Other Clients' Case Histories

Matthew: "On each soul retrieval I was able to tell initially that something entered my body. Over the next day few days I was able to notice a more complete feeling within myself and that I would be able to interact with others on more levels that I had in the past. Looking back over four years later from the soul retrievals, I can say that it does not solve all problems but it does allow you to go through life with a full deck. This makes things much easier. Most of the parts had traits that helped fit into areas that were already present so the biggest gain was just being more present in the situation. Also it brings more completeness in each everyday moment, which increases the enjoyment one experiences from living."

Honey: "During the soul retrieval and transformation process I somehow reclaimed memories of various episodes and a six-year history of being molested by a neighbor. I saw how my soul parts had fragmented and left. I don't recall the "how's" of recovery, but I began to feel myself healing and the parts becoming available to me again. I felt a wholeness unknown to me for years. Maryphyllis walked me through the broken places and helped me become a whole person.

"Now, many years later, life is better and I have a much clearer understanding of what I need to do to keep it that way.""

Zanya Alpha: "In 2003 I came to MaryPhyllis for a soul retrieval to address the issue of self-doubt. I grew up in a critical environment that was not a safe place to express or be myself. I learned to doubt my own inner guidance. Before the soul retrieval I was thinking like a victim, feeling helpless about things in my life. I believed that I was to put other people's needs before my own and would focus on trying to make others happy. Then I would resent it when I felt exhausted or didn't get something finished that was important to me. While at the same time of treating myself like I didn't matter, I also was feeling driven to learn and accomplish new skills and knowledge. It seemed the more I tried to take a step toward my goals, something would always intervene and sabotage my efforts. I'm in my 40's and more reflective about my life; what has been my experience is that not only do these issues not go away on their own, but they become amplified.

"The soul retrieval returned four soul parts that dealt with evidencing my own truth, connection to my soul, grounding, the substance of my being (core of who I am), working with Nature Spirits. The soul retrieval and transformation process has given me the needed reinforcement to begin the difficult work of changing deeply seated patterns and beliefs that have been blocks in my life since childhood.

After the soul retrieval, I began to feel more guided. I have more clarity and focus on responsibility for my well being. My journal writing became less whiney and began focusing on the things I want to do with my life. When I did need to work through a problem, a wise voice appeared sometimes identifying itself as one of the soul parts or would be a "we" and would give me clarity and perspective on the situation. I occasionally see a glowing ball of light dart across the room (nature spirits?). I am continuing to learn to pay attention to what I feel and to ask myself what I need and what makes me happy. I have more hope despite setbacks and disappointments.

"I still have more soul retrieval work to do. But I feel that what I've done so far has moved me forward and on the path that I want to be on. For me, it's hard but highly worth it because I feel that I'm building the foundation to stand on for the rest of my life."

Suzanne: "I had several soul retrievals and integrations and found them to be wonderful and helpful. When the soul parts were first returned to me by Maryphyllis, I felt full and very happy to have them with me again. Maryphyllis then gently guided me through some difficult integrations of soul parts that carried painful memories for me that I had not yet dealt with. (The soul parts had left to take away some of the painful memories for me so that I could go on with life. But, I had to have them back so that I could be more fully present in my life.) I was able to reclaim and heal the pain from those memories and move forward more clearly and with more strength in my life. It also helped me to set appropriate boundaries with some of the people responsible for these traumas.

"During one of my soul retrievals, I gained back many different soul parts that left at different times in my life all due to a lack of self-acceptance. This has been a major theme in my life and having those several soul parts back enabled me to get back many of the qualities I had also lost with each of those soul parts. I also got back some of the anger of those soul parts for having been treated as if I were not a valuable person as a child, and Maryphyllis helped me deal with this, also. Maryphyllis always had the right thing to say (from Spirit) during the transformation sessions that helped me to truly embrace and love those missing parts of myself. I became much more whole and self-accepting as a result of this process.

"I had another transformation session where Maryphyllis asked me to go to the core of my being. Within the shamanic journey I found that my core was all covered up with crackly brown parchment paper and it was difficult to get to. I slowly removed the paper to find that there was a big emerald there. I realized that I had covered up a very important and valuable part of myself that was now revealed.

"Since these sessions, it has been a couple of years. I have really needed and enjoyed the self-acceptance and deeper connection with the inner core of myself. I was finally able to see myself as important enough to take care of myself and began practicing yoga and walking around my neighborhood right after the transformation work. Then, over time, I was able to care for myself enough to take the time to go to the gym six days a week to exercise. I even hired a personal trainer! I started eating healthfully and really caring for myself on a deeper level, instead of putting everyone else (parents, children, husband, friends – everyone!) first and myself very last on the list, or not even on the list at all. I eventually was able to lose the weight that I had been trying unsuccessfully to lose for about fourteen years. I accept myself enough now to realize that a few pounds may need to stay with me for a little while longer. That's now okay, whereas it wasn't, prior to those soul retrievals and transformations."

Rosehart: "Before experiencing several soul retrievals from Maryphyllis, I lived my life with various gaps. Without knowing exactly what was missing, for many years I felt confusion, terrible fearfulness, and something missing in different areas of my emotional self. In particular, I felt there was a huge hole in my heart.

"Before the last work we did in 2005, the feeling of being overwhelmed and trapped by my relationship with my mother had reached unmanageable proportions, even though we lived 3000 miles apart. I felt that I was being smothered by my relationship with my mother. After our last work together, I immediately felt joyful wholeness; it was transforming. I not only felt like my heart was whole again, literally, but I felt a great compassion for my mother that has stayed with me, enabling me to experience a healthy relationship with her for the first time since I was a child. Friends noted that I was much calmer and more focused in many areas of my life. The change in me was so dramatic that I began a quest to discover my true name, Rosehart.

"Now I am able to set boundaries with my mother and to love her, without feeling smothered by her love. The transformation process was critical. A soul retrieval I did with another practitioner did not include the transformation process. It also did not have the sense of completeness; the relationship between my father and me was not properly healed. I know that there is more work to be done on this soul part, using the full transformation process that I learned from Maryphyllis in 2005."

Lyn: Lyn's primary concerns when she first came to me for soul retrievals in 1998 were Chronic Fatigue Syndrome and life-long shyness. Over a seven-year span, we worked with various facets of these issues, using soul retrieval, soul transformation, past-life healing, ancestral lines clearing and numerous other modalities.

Now, in 2008, she says her energy levels are a lot better although she still has to be careful about what she does. At the emotional, mental and spiritual levels she is very happy. She cannot imagine being the person she was before; even trying to think of "that person" evokes a sense of being much removed, like witnessing someone in a movie. She has compassion for "that woman" then, but she feels very different now.

The essence of herself in 1998 was of a four-year-old soul part in a blue dress, shy and scared. Through loving her, she realized she was loving herself. Gaining self-love, she began to see the world through the lens of love rather than of fear. Developing self-love opened her to ongoing spiritual growth.

Epilogue: Lasting Effects?

Through all of our work together, and particularly with soul retrieval/transformation, she has become more aware that everything in life is an opportunity for soul growth. She learned how to work continuously, through *all* experiences, not just with soul retrieval itself. Soul retrieval opens an avenue of awareness that all life is one of growth. Soul retrieval and soul transformation remove barriers. But that's just the beginning.

Anna: "When I first saw Maryphyllis' ad in a health and spiritual magazine some of the symptoms she described as a possible sign of soul loss interested me: pervasive fears, difficulty concentrating, and difficulty acting on thoughts. I did have some doubts about engaging a shaman because shamanism seemed to have become popularized, i.e., not seemingly genuine. Through the years I had decided to keep my Christian faith as a guide in the world of New Age, to steer out of the most dubious therapies and views. In addition I had a wonderful legacy from my mother to explore the spiritual world and healing as a way of self-help.

"I had been engaged in my own spiritual growth for twenty years and had tried different therapies, including psychotherapy, to work with my issues and my struggle in life. In psychotherapy I explored the relationships of my childhood. Especially one relationship had come with such strong expectations, that I had redefined myself to adjust. I felt I had made a lot of progress and had come to stable ground in my life. I have a strong and happy marriage, which is a good center point in my life, and we have two wonderful kids. Still, there was an inner struggle to cope with the natural expectations of life because parts of me had a pattern of just wanting to adjust and silence my inner longing.

"I often felt anxious about the smallest things. Some situations that naturally occur in everyday life got me obsessed and drained my energy. I was easily stressed. I had doubts about myself and my life and a nagging fear that everything would suddenly change, for the worse.

"I had started my own writing some years back and I wanted to pursue this. I had good ideas, I tried, I wrote, I got some pieces finalized, but still felt like I could not materialize what it was I really wanted to do. I got pretty close and focused, but it felt as if I could not grab it, pull it down and make it mine.

"At times this inner struggle made me grumpy, sometimes nasty to my family, tired, gloomy and this would easily distress joyful times. I felt an inability to stay focused and to materialize my ideas, and these were my main issues when consulting Maryphyllis. Should I try this other thing, yet another kind of therapy that will help me for a while, but may just as well leave me in the same limbo anyway?

"Still, I felt guidance from within and knew to go for it when I had this feeling in my heart. I felt instant trust and relief when I made the appointment and also for the process Maryphyllis described. She asked me to learn how to do shamanic journeying, to find my power animal. I was aware of my spiritual teacher and also of an animal that I felt was "with me". However I had not learned how to communicate with them. The shamanic journeying was just the right thing to do. It felt like a meditation in my own personal inner world, very safe and strangely familiar.

"When it was time for the soul retrieval I was a little nervous. I was worried that my old issues would become too sensitive and disturbing again, even if Maryphyllis assured me that it did not have to be that way. It was so nice to just sit there and be open, as Maryphyllis asked of me, and let the work be done by her. In other therapies there usually was a struggle on the personal level to reach within, but this was something done for me, a precious gift. There were three soul parts that came back to me and Maryphyllis described them to me in pictures that I immediately accepted in my mind and heart. It was a joy! I felt awed that these beautiful essences were a part of me! These soul parts had character traits that I had longed for, for so many years. And here I learned that they actually did exist, and that they would be back and be a part of me!

"Well, the journeying at home to get to know my soul parts and to get the integration process prepared went well. Getting to know my soul parts was a delightful process, as was learning what they asked of me: awareness and some changes. The needs of my soul parts were possible to incorporate in my everyday life. For example, one of my soul parts needs me to do beautiful things: make myself beautiful, cook beautiful food and be aware of what is beautiful around me. In addition I need to find a space within and around me that is without fear and doubt; this was also something this soul part could help me with. It seems logical since beauty is the opposite of fear. Still, this was a challenge, since fear and doubt had been a part of my attitude and my once redefined personality for so long.

Epilogue: Lasting Effects?

"Those old patterns of behavior had to change, for me and my soul part to stay happy. How this happened was that I had a day of doubt and fear. I questioned myself, the soul retrieval process and the reasons for it – was I fooling myself? Who knows what's real anyway? Yet I experienced this objectively, like it was a stage show of what fear and doubt are. The thoughts didn't disturb me to the core, like anxiety used to do. I experienced these feelings as they were, yet didn't feel them as an essential part of me. They existed outside of me. It's like going in to a very dirty restroom, you have an urgent need to get rid of, but you don't have to stay and you can (and will) choose another, cleaner, restroom next time! To live and not doubt myself is a new experience. I hesitated to expect things from myself, since this has been a sensitive point within me. On the other hand, if I don't doubt myself and my abilities, what is possible to do!?

"In this process I learned by experience that it is possible to choose not to have fear and doubt. So now if I experience a situation that really triggers this old pattern, I do let the fear appear so that I can see what it is and then I explore that. Then I think the opposite and know that, yes, there may also be another outcome of the situation. Then I let go of the fear. It really is that easy and simple. Previously I would have let the fear get in to me, grow and make me anxious. Now I just choose it to go away. I believe that the doubt within me has been the main reason for my issue of not being able to focus on what I want to do so that I can materialize it. And the doubts, in turn, come from having been "taught" an urge to adjust to others' expectations of me; or rather that being me is not enough. It has taken some time to explore this different me!

"This process has helped me profoundly and in so many unexpected ways! What first appeared like small inner changes have an outcome in everyday life that feels huge. I am surprised when I stand up for myself in various situations. I now speak my concern at once. Before I used to first think and think about it, let it eat me, get anxious – and then the moment to speak up was gone and I never got the concern out of my system. I do believe this change has come about because my soul parts are now back and help me achieve it. This has give me a permanent change!

"I still have three or four more core soul parts to retrieve. I am deeply thankful to this opportunity. Now half a year after my first ceremony, I feel ready to continue finding me!"

Epilogue: Lasting Effects?

"Final" Words

It is exciting and uplifting to witness each person's unique experience of this wonderful healing work. We are here to grow spiritually. My over-all sense of the work of soul retrieval and transformation is that it helps the individual to become more and more the Light of Spirit within, which each of us essentially is. It is my joy to share all of this with you, that you too can take part in it.

ABOUT

MARY

PHYLLIS

HORN

Maryphyllis' Educational Background

Maryphyllis received her B.A. in music education from Gettysburg College, Pennsylvania, and her M.Ed. in music education from The Pennsylvania State University, PA. For 31 years she taught public high school award-winning choral music in New York State, South Carolina and New Mexico. During this time she began studying metaphysical and holistic topics, graduated from Connie Newton's Integrated Awareness program, became a Reiki practitioner, and enrolled in Sancta Sophia Seminary in Tahlequah, Oklahoma. After three years of study at this interfaith, metaphysical seminary, she received her metaphysical ministry ordination in 1987.

In 1993 she left her teaching career, to attend The Naropa Institute in Boulder, Colorado, for a Master's degree study of Transpersonal Psychology. It was there that she experienced a profound mystical calling to shamanism. Within a few months' time she took Michael Harner's Basic Shamanism workshop, Sandra Ingerman's Soul Retrieval seminar and various other pertinent studies from the Foundation for Shamanic Studies. She also received certification in spiritual hypnotherapy through the Alchemical Hypnotherapy Institute of Colorado.

Maryphyllis' Shamanic Practice

In 1995 she moved to Pittsboro, North Carolina, and set up a private practice in shamanic counseling and healing, along with hypnotherapy work. Since then, she has studied additional healing modalities, each one for the purpose of being better able to help her clients' healing. Her certifications include Pastoral Counseling from Sancta Sophia Seminary, Thought Field Therapy, Past-Life Regression from Dolores Cannon (hypnotherapist in Arkansas), and Genonetics (Karmic Matrix Clearing is a shamanic derivative of this). She has studied Feng Shui with Sue Ruzicka (Feng Shui Master in Tennessee) and others, and became a Reconnection Level III practitioner with Dr. Eric Pearl of California.

Her in-depth study of various forms of depossession have led her to the hypnotherapy style of Irene Hickman (hypnotherapist in Illinois), the shamanic style of Betsy Bergstrom (shamanic practitioner in Washington state), and an intuitive style of Diana Henderson and Julia Hanline (healing practitioners in North Carolina).

Maryphyllis' Calling

Maryphyllis' primary calling within the shamanic work is to help people get in touch with their inner guidance, to help them mend their soul through soul retrieval and soul transformation, and to help them heal their past so that they can tap into their individual missions when they are ready to do so. Clearing the past may include past-life therapy, chakra healing, ancestral lines clearing, depossession and more.

Her study with human teachers has formed but a small part of her spiritual training. Since embarking on the shamanic path in 1994, the vast majority of her instruction has been from her own spirit helpers, aka power animals and spirit teachers. As part of helping her heal herself, they have given her volumes of insights and methods to help others heal themselves. Ancestral Lines Clearing and information in this book are but a small portion of those gifts from Spirit.

BIBLIOGRAPHY

BOOKS

Eliade, Mircea. SHAMANISM, ARCHAIC TECHNIQUES OF ECSTACY. Bollingen Series LXXVI. Princeton University Press, NJ. 1964.

Harner, Michael. THE WAY OF THE SHAMAN. Bantam New Age Books, USA. 1982.

Ingerman, Sandra. SOUL RETRIEVAL: MENDING THE FRAGMENTED SELF. Harper Collins Pub., San Francisco, CA. 1991.

RESOURCES

THE FOUNDATION FOR SHAMANIC STUDIES, P.O.Box 1939, Mill Valley, CA 94942. www.shamanism.org

THE SOCIETY FOR SHAMANIC PRACTITIONERS, 2300 8th Street, Olivenhain, CA 92024 www.shamansociety.org

THE ASSOCIATION FOR RESEARCH AND ENLIGHTENMENT (A.R.E.), 215 67th Street, Virginia Beach, VA 23451-2061. www.are-cayce.com

SANCTA SOPHIA SEMINARY, 22 Summit Ridge Drive, Tahlequah, OK 74464 www.sanctasophia.org

Bibliography

INDEX

Index

Index

32240478R00084

Made in the USA
San Bernardino, CA
12 April 2019